AZERBAIJAN: U.S. ENERGY, SECURITY, AND HUMAN RIGHTS INTERESTS

HEARING

BEFORE THE

SUBCOMMITTEE ON EUROPE, EURASIA, AND EMERGING THREATS

OF THE

COMMITTEE ON FOREIGN AFFAIRS
HOUSE OF REPRESENTATIVES

ONE HUNDRED FOURTEENTH CONGRESS

FIRST SESSION

FEBRUARY 12, 2015

Serial No. 114–6

Printed for the use of the Committee on Foreign Affairs

Available via the World Wide Web: http://www.foreignaffairs.house.gov/ or
http://www.gpo.gov/fdsys/

U.S. GOVERNMENT PUBLISHING OFFICE

93–285PDF   WASHINGTON : 2015

For sale by the Superintendent of Documents, U.S. Government Publishing Office
Internet: bookstore.gpo.gov   Phone: toll free (866) 512–1800; DC area (202) 512–1800
Fax: (202) 512–2104   Mail: Stop IDCC, Washington, DC 20402–0001

COMMITTEE ON FOREIGN AFFAIRS

EDWARD R. ROYCE, California, *Chairman*

CHRISTOPHER H. SMITH, New Jersey
ILEANA ROS-LEHTINEN, Florida
DANA ROHRABACHER, California
STEVE CHABOT, Ohio
JOE WILSON, South Carolina
MICHAEL T. McCAUL, Texas
TED POE, Texas
MATT SALMON, Arizona
DARRELL E. ISSA, California
TOM MARINO, Pennsylvania
JEFF DUNCAN, South Carolina
MO BROOKS, Alabama
PAUL COOK, California
RANDY K. WEBER SR., Texas
SCOTT PERRY, Pennsylvania
RON DeSANTIS, Florida
MARK MEADOWS, North Carolina
TED S. YOHO, Florida
CURT CLAWSON, Florida
SCOTT DesJARLAIS, Tennessee
REID J. RIBBLE, Wisconsin
DAVID A. TROTT, Michigan
LEE M. ZELDIN, New York
TOM EMMER, Minnesota

ELIOT L. ENGEL, New York
BRAD SHERMAN, California
GREGORY W. MEEKS, New York
ALBIO SIRES, New Jersey
GERALD E. CONNOLLY, Virginia
THEODORE E. DEUTCH, Florida
BRIAN HIGGINS, New York
KAREN BASS, California
WILLIAM KEATING, Massachusetts
DAVID CICILLINE, Rhode Island
ALAN GRAYSON, Florida
AMI BERA, California
ALAN S. LOWENTHAL, California
GRACE MENG, New York
LOIS FRANKEL, Florida
TULSI GABBARD, Hawaii
JOAQUIN CASTRO, Texas
ROBIN L. KELLY, Illinois
BRENDAN F. BOYLE, Pennsylvania

AMY PORTER, *Chief of Staff*   THOMAS SHEEHY, *Staff Director*
JASON STEINBAUM, *Democratic Staff Director*

––––––––––

SUBCOMMITTEE ON EUROPE, EURASIA, AND EMERGING THREATS

DANA ROHRABACHER, California, *Chairman*

TED POE, Texas
TOM MARINO, Pennsylvania
MO BROOKS, Alabama
PAUL COOK, California
RANDY K. WEBER SR., Texas
REID J. RIBBLE, Wisconsin
DAVID A. TROTT, Michigan

GREGORY W. MEEKS, New York
ALBIO SIRES, New Jersey
THEODORE E. DEUTCH, Florida
WILLIAM KEATING, Massachusetts
LOIS FRANKEL, Florida
TULSI GABBARD, Hawaii

(II)

CONTENTS

AZERBAIJAN: U.S. ENERGY, SECURITY, AND HUMAN RIGHTS INTERESTS

THURSDAY, FEBRUARY 12, 2015

House of Representatives,
Subcommittee on Europe, Eurasia, and Emerging Threats,
Committee on Foreign Affairs,
Washington, DC.

The subcommittee met, pursuant to notice, at 1 o'clock p.m., in room 2200 Rayburn House Office Building, Hon. Dana Rohrabacher (chairman of the subcommittee) presiding.

Mr. ROHRABACHER. The subcommittee is called to order.

This is the inaugural meeting of the Europe, Eurasia, and Emerging Threats Subcommittee for the 114th Congress. I am happy to introduce our new ranking member, Greg Meeks of New York. I am sure that we will have a very productive session together in these next 2 years.

So, we are very happy to have you with us, Gregory.

Before I go into my opening statement, I want to recognize that we are joined in the audience by Sarah Paulsworth—Sarah, where are you?—and Sarah's husband Emin, and I am going to pronounce this, Heseynov, who helped to found the Azeri NGO dedicated to journalist safety. When it became clear that he was wanted by the authorities, he asked the United States Embassy for help. Our Embassy turned him away, but he was granted safe haven in the Swiss Embassy, where he is today. And again, I guess it is a sad day when the Swiss are more courageous than the Americans.

Our topic for this afternoon is the U.S. relationship with Azerbaijan, a country of about 9 million people on the coast of the Caspian Sea, sandwiched between Iran, Russia, Armenia, Georgia, and Turkey, a pretty tough neighborhood.

Our relationship with Azerbaijan is normally described as being comprised of three parts: Energy, security, and human rights. Azerbaijan is rich in oil and natural gas. Since the 1990s, it has grown into a notable exporter of oil, which is making Azerbaijan a relatively and notably wealthy country.

Now, with the construction of the Southern Gas Corridor, Azerbaijan has the potential to play a key role in helping to provide the European Union with sources of natural gas that is not controlled by Russia.

The Azerbaijani Government has been a source of irreplaceable support for the United States and NATO operations in Afghanistan. Azerbaijan is a key link in the northern distribution network which supplies and carries troops battling in Afghanistan.

(1)

On this point, I would like to mention especially I want to thank the Azerbaijani Government for their cooperation in saving the lives of numerous U.S. military personnel. While acknowledging this important context, it is impossible to overlook Azerbaijan's poor track record when it comes to civil liberties. Azerbaijan, as I say, is in a very tough neighborhood and borders on other countries—this is important—it borders on other countries that have far worse human rights records. But human rights violations in one country does not justify or excuse them in another country. So, we need to keep these in perspective on both sides of that argument.

The disturbing reports of 90-plus political prisoners held by the Azerbaijani Government just can't be ignored. It would be better for all concerned if the Azerbaijani Government, which has many attributes which we are putting into our calculation, but it would certainly be better for all of us—these attributes also include what, freedom of religion and other important elements. Of course, it would be a really good thing if the Azerbaijani government wasn't so thin-skinned about criticism because that leads them to actions that really are unacceptable and unnecessary, causing all of us problems, including themselves.

The purpose of this hearing is not—I repeat not—to unfairly bash Azerbaijan. But disregarding its shortcomings will not improve the situation, as was evident the other day when, after Christmas in Azerbaijan, the authorities raided and shut down the Baku Bureau of Radio Free Europe and Radio Liberty. That was, of course, shutting Radio Liberty and Radio Free Europe is just unacceptable.

I, myself, have advocated, for example, that the same Azeri language service that we are talking about that was used in Radio Liberty and Radio Free Europe, that that same Azeri language service covered northern Iran and has serviced the Azeri people in Iran. The Baku Bureau and its employees should be released and be free to go about their work.

Again, the purpose of this hearing is not to attack or bash Azerbaijan. It serves everyone's interest to recognize the many positive aspects of our relationship with Azerbaijan and the great potential that Azerbaijan has to play a positive role, and it is already playing a positive regional role. This positive role in that region will have significance for the entire planet.

There is a legitimate fear, for example, of radical Islamic's subterfuge of Azeri society and Azeri government. Unfortunately, repressing democratic elements in any society increases the appeal that such radicals have. So, it is in no one's best interest to being thin-skinned about criticism and to act against people who are criticizing your government for whatever reason.

The people of Azerbaijan are not fanatics and neither is their government. They have much to be proud of, but flaws that should not be ignored.

I look forward to hearing from the panel today and hope that their conversation with us will leave us with some constructive recommendations of how we can improve our relations with Azerbaijan and how Azerbaijan can improve their relations with us.

I would hope that, without objection, all members will have at least 5 legislative days to submit additional questions or extraneous materials for the record.

Before recognizing Mr. Meeks for his opening statement, I would like to recognize that we have a very special guest with us. We have one whose husband is, of course, being held in Azerbaijan. We wish him well and hope that maybe this hearing could say we are friends; let this guy go, please.

We also have a wonderful other good friend, Dan Burton—there he is—Dan Burton, who actually chaired this committee a couple of years ago and has been a dear friend to all of us and one of the most hard-working and responsible Members of Congress that I met in my 26 years here. He is a fine man.

Dan, we are very, very pleased that you have come here to observe what we are doing today.

With that said, Mr. Meeks, please feel free to have your opening statement.

Mr. MEEKS. Thank you, Mr. Chairman.

I look forward to working with you over the next 2 years. We have done some traveling together, and I think that we will be working collectively together to try to stay focused on the issues of this subcommittee. You know, I look forward to working with you and our colleagues on both sides of the aisle on the important issues that fall under the subcommittee's jurisdiction.

In this subcommittee it is up to us to ensure that American interests in Europe and Eurasia are protected and promoted, but also that the common ideals and interests that we share with our allies and partners in the region are held to the highest standards. It is an honor to take up the ranking member role during these trying times in the region.

Azerbaijan has a remarkable and notable history. Well before Azerbaijan gained independence in 1991, it made an important and global distinction when it became, albeit briefly, one of the world's first Muslim democratic republics.

Since then, Azerbaijan has had significant success in navigating the difficult path to becoming an open-market economy. But success does not come without concern in other areas.

I believe our witnesses today will highlight some of the areas of concern, including human rights and the lack of democratic governance. But I hope we can also discuss ways in which the United States can support progress. I hope we can talk about the broader scope of cooperation with the EU and OSCE on some of the challenges.

Human rights and democracy advancements will not happen in a vacuum, and we must work in a multilateral way to support progress. The U.S.-Azerbaijan relationship is a partnership that we value. Azerbaijan is a critically-located partner in the South Caucasus Region. It is a secular nation that neighbors Iran and works closely with the United States. That is not an easy position to be in. It borders Russia and is the key to the EU on energy diversification. In short, our partnership is not one we can take for granted.

Today's hearing is for me an opportunity to examine the tough issues and potential for advancement in the nation that I believe has promise. Azerbaijan's success is, of course, broadened by its natural resources. But I know that our Government is also committed to helping Azerbaijan grow the non-oil sectors of the economy to avoid overreliance.

We are also committed to fostering a vibrant, open society and upholding democratic ideals as a part of the development process. We want to build on Azerbaijan's success in using its resources, its resource wealth, to reduce poverty levels dramatically and grow its middle class and create jobs.

Ensuring the continued success of Azerbaijan's development and encouraging democratic progress is of strategic importance to the United States. Our interests on all fronts are critically linked. The energy and security cooperation we enjoy is important. But these things are not separate and apart from the equally-important need to ensure that we address civil society's push for an open and democratic society.

I hope to hear from our experts today on the recent setbacks in this area. President Aliyev and the Azerbaijan Government should know that we are concerned with the treatment of several members of the Azeri civil society.

I know that progress is not always linear and not often

as quick as we would like. In fact, right here in the United States we are still perfecting our democracy and our great nation. And we took too long, in my estimate, in this country to correct some of our own human rights mistakes. But what we want to do is work together to share methods to make sure all voices are respected.

So, I look forward to a fruitful discussion where we can explore what we in Congress can offer and do to positive growth in Azerbaijan that includes all members of its society, for it is a very important ally, and we do need to work collectively together to make life better for all of our people and our citizens.

And I yield back.

Mr. ROHRABACHER. Thank you, Mr. Meeks.

If any other member of the hearing panel would like to—Mr. Sires, maybe a 1- or 2-minute opening statement—feel free.

Mr. SIRES. Thank you, Mr. Chairman, for today's hearing on Azerbaijan. Thank you for being here today.

Since Azerbaijan broke free of the Soviet Union over two decades ago, the U.S. has had a concerted interest in strengthening democracy in Azerbaijan. Azerbaijan is unique, as it is a bridge between the East and the West. A peaceful, democratic, and prosperous Azerbaijan is in the best interest of the United States and our European allies.

Unfortunately, there have been many obstacles to a fully-recognized democracy in Azerbaijan, including ongoing government corruption and human rights abuses. I am deeply troubled by recent efforts by the government to crack down on civil society groups and independent media. As we all know, a democracy cannot exist without the ability of the citizens to freely exercise their voices.

I look forward to hearing from our esteemed panel of witnesses on how Congress can shape policies that will assist in promoting democratic principles in Azerbaijan in order to strengthen our ties in the region.

Thank you, and I yield back.

Mr. ROHRABACHER. Thank you.

Mr. Deutch, do you have an opening statement?

Mr. DEUTCH. I do. Thank you. Thank you, Chairman Rohrabacher and Ranking Member Meeks.

I am honored to rejoin this subcommittee which covers a region with significant value for our national security and one that is facing many new and significant threats, and Azerbaijan is no exception to this. It is easy to understand what risks the country faces just by looking at its precarious geographic location with Russia to its north, which has shown irredentist actions toward its neighbors. To its south is Iran, a state sponsor of terrorism with nuclear weapons ambitions and a significant Azeri population. And Azerbaijan also shares a border with Armenia, with the unresolved Nagorno-Karabakh region in between.

Azerbaijan has built up a multifaceted partnership with European countries and the United States. Its access to offshore ore deposits and the plan to build a pipeline via Turkey to southern Europe is an appealing prospect for many European countries as an alternative source to Russia's near monopoly as an energy provider to eastern Europe.

Amid the list of threats coming out of Europe and the Middle East, our security and counterterrorism cooperation is of significant mutual value. That cooperation doesn't prevent us, in fact, nothing should prevent us from speaking out for human rights. And the human rights situation in Azerbaijan cannot be overlooked.

NGOs are being intimidated and shuttered. Free media and journalism is being inhibited, and pro-democracy leaders are being incarcerated at alarming rates. Last December, Security Forces raided and shut down the Radio Free Europe/Radio Liberty office in Baku, and other U.S. programs like Peace Corps are closing shop.

Regressive human rights policies like these are concerning. When it gets to the point that international civil society groups which are active in countries, in order to improve the democratic and human rights climate, are forced to pull back their presence out of fear of oppression and incarceration, it should send a loud signal to the government that its policies are heading in the wrong direction.

The LGBT community, in particular, experiences a tremendous amount of social stigma, often in the form of physical abuse and harassment. And with restricted registration policies for civil society organizations, Azerbaijan is left with zero groups promoting the rights of LGBT people in the form of legal protections and public acceptance.

These are important questions for Congress to ask. I thank the chairman for holding this public hearing.

And I hope you will accept my apologies. I have two other hearings taking place at exactly the same moment. So, I will be back——

Mr. ROHRABACHER. How is it possible that somebody has two hearings at the same time? It almost always happens, the one you really want to go to—and you have got to go to them—and then, all of a sudden, there are three others scheduled.

Well, thank you for joining us and sharing your thoughts with us, at least to kick it off today.

So, we have three great witnesses today. First is Dr. Audrey Altstadt. I think is that the pronunciation? I am sorry if I got it wrong. Dr. Altstadt is a professor at the University of Massachusetts, Amherst, and currently spending a year in Washington as a Fellow at the Wilson Center.

She has authored dozens of articles on Azerbaijan and has been following the issues in that country since the 1980s. She earned her PhD from the University of Chicago and is currently writing a book about Azerbaijan.

We also have with us Ambassador Richard Kauzlarich—okay, that is good enough?—the Director of the Center for Energy Science and Policy at George Mason University. He has held a number of high-level positions within the State Department, including formerly being our Ambassador to Azerbaijan and Bosnia-Herzegovina. He also served as the National Intelligence Officer for Europe on the National Intelligence Council.

Finally, we have Dr. Svante Cornell. He is the Director of Central Asia-Caucasus Institute and the Silk Road Studies Program at Johns Hopkins University. He is the author of four books and many articles on security studies and international relations. He is an expert on the Caucasus and earned his PhD from the University of Uppsala in Sweden.

I am really bad on some of these foreign names. But Uppsala, all right.

Listen, we welcome our witnesses, and we thank you for sharing your expertise with us today. I would ask if you could keep it down to 5 minutes and the rest for the record. You are certainly welcome to submit as long a statement as you want for the record. And then, we will follow up with questions after you have all testified.

So, Doctor, you may proceed.

STATEMENT OF AUDREY ALTSTADT, PH.D., FELLOW, KENNAN INSTITUTE, WOODROW WILSON INTERNATIONAL CENTER FOR SCHOLARS

Ms. ALTSTADT. Thank you for the opportunity to be here today. I appreciate the fact that we are having this meeting.

Azerbaijan is the only country that borders both Russia and Iran. It was ruled by both and it bears the vestiges of both in its politics and its culture. Its oil and gas wealth have made Azerbaijan a significant contributor to European energy security and gives it the potential to be an important partner in this and other commercial dealings.

The government has cooperated with the United States in the war on terror. At the same time, the Government of Azerbaijan must deal with pressures from its neighbors and near neighbors, and these are challenges that any government in Baku would have to face, by virtue of its location.

Azerbaijan's independence and internal stability are necessary, but not sufficient, for it to be a full and healthy functioning partner as a state or a society. Nor does stability alone make it a good partner.

Azerbaijan today is not a democracy and its government does not respect human rights. The present government has been moving away from, and not closer to, pluralism, democratic elections, open discourse in society, freely-functioning media, and the observation of human rights. These restrictions have gradually increased over the last 10 years, but most radically so in the last 1½ to 2 years, since the Presidential election campaign of 2013. It has become worst of all since the spring and summer of 2014.

Ruling circles have shown intolerance of criticism and protests. Yet, the criticism and protests have continued, raising fears of a potential Baku Maidan, as we have seen in Ukraine.

The government of President Ilham Aliyev has carried out a pre-emptive strike against regime critics of political groups and parties, especially youth movements, human rights defenders, journalists, and the lawyers that defend them. These people are not against Azerbaijan's statehood, independence, or stability, but do oppose the ruling regime's policies and, increasingly, the ruling regime itself.

The crackdown of 2014 is counterproductive and dangerous. Public discourse in civil society is the life breath of the body politic. Constricting the space for freedom of speech, assembly, and press, as we have seen in Azerbaijan, is suffocating to that body. The loser is Azerbaijan society, which is deprived of political participation and peaceful redress of grievances.

But the government also loses because it is deprived of new ideas, the purifying fire of public debate, and the legitimacy which transparency bestows. Such restrictions, moreover, can drive the populace toward radicalism in its effort to find a venue for social and economic change.

The European Parliament, the United States Subcommittee on Human Rights, and a number of other international and non-governmental organizations have noted this disturbing trend in the last year and more. The Council of Europe Commissioner for Human Rights said, ''All of my partners in Azerbaijan are in jail.''

The rhetoric of these repressions has taken a decidedly anti-American tone. In December, an article was published by the Presidential Chief of Staff, Ramiz Mehtiyev, which accused the United States of instigating color revolutions in Georgia and Ukraine, the Arab Spring, and the Maidan movement in Ukraine. He accused the U.S. of trying to destabilize the Aliyev government under the guise of protecting human rights.

The alleged U.S. tools were NGOs and Azerbaijani citizens that Mehtiyev declared to be a fifth column within Azerbaijan. Such citizens, he added, were disloyal, and he named as one example Investigative Journalist Khadija Ismayilova who worked at Radio Liberty in Baku. Two days later, she was arrested, and by the end of the month, as we have noted here, the Radio Liberty, or Azadliq Radiosu, office in Baku was raided and closed, and its staff was questioned multiple times without an attorney being present.

These statements and actions within Azerbaijan suggest that the Azerbaijani Government may be moving away from the West and increasingly toward Russia, which President Aliyev has recently called ''a good friend.'' It may be that a pro-Russian faction is in the ascendency, but it could not act without President Aliyev's knowledge and approval.

This does not mean, however, that Azerbaijan's leaders are completely changing direction. It is more likely that they are seeking a new balance among neighbors and business partners. Baku's ruling elites do not want to lose the benefits of commercial deals with the West and the lavish lifestyle options available in western countries, including real estate, education for their children, and bank accounts in stable currencies protected by law.

Azerbaijan's elites want to maintain these opportunities and privileges that the West offers and present themselves as western partners without actually fulfilling the obligations of a western state, a member of the OSCE and the Council of Europe, a country that observes human rights and holds free and fair elections. In short, they want to have it both ways.

The United States should certainly evaluate Azerbaijan in a nuanced, holistic, and realistic light, but it is imperative that the United States not ignore or deny the Azerbaijan's regimes failings in human rights, media freedom, civil society and democratization.

The U.S. owes it to the pro-democracy forces within Azerbaijan to speak up clearly and consistently for the defense of the same rights that are the foundations of the United States. The argument that the U.S. should set aside these failings in the interests of commercial gain or so-called stability, which the regime advertises, would constitute a betrayal of U.S. values and would further diminish the image and the moral power of the United States in Azerbaijan and in the world.

Thank you.

[The prepared statement of Ms. Altstadt follows:]

"Azerbaijan: US Energy, Security and Human Rights Interests,"
Testimony of Dr. Audrey L. Altstadt
Fellow, Kennan Institute, Woodrow Wilson Center
Professor of History, University of Massachusetts, Amherst

Europe, Eurasia and Emerging Threats Subcommittee
House Foreign Affairs Committee
February 12, 2015

<u>Executive Summary:</u>

Azerbaijan is an energy-rich post-Soviet state situated between Russia and Iran. Its oil and gas wealth contribute to European energy security. Its strategic location is relevant to combating illegal drug and arms trade, human trafficking, and terrorism. Post-Soviet Azerbaijan has joined the OSCE and aided the US in the War on Terror.

Azerbaijan today is not a democracy. The government has been moving away from, not closer to, pluralism and democratic elections. Critics of the regime are harassed or go to jail. The trend accelerated in 2014. There are about 100 political prisoners in Azerbaijani jails including human rights defenders, journalists and lawyers. Corruption remains an obstacle to social trust and economic integration into the West.

Government officials have recently expressed anti-American views. The president's chief of staff Ramiz Mehtiyev accused the US of trying to "destabilize" the Aliyev government under the guise of protecting human rights. US-funded NGOs are under attack and Radio Liberty was closed in late December.

<u>Recommendations</u>: Evaluate Azerbaijan in a more nuanced, holistic, and realistic light, acknowledging its strategic and economic importance, but also identifying the shortcomings in democracy indicators, restrictions on civil society including the media and human rights activists. The US owes it to the pro-democracy forces within Azerbaijan to speak up clearly for the defense of the same rights that are the foundation of the United States. The US can assist Azerbaijan in defeating corruption and cultivating civil society as means to strengthen that country, allow fruitful political discourse, and reduce the appeal of radicalism.

Analysis:

Azerbaijan is an energy-rich post-Soviet state situated between Russia and Iran. It is located in a geopolitically and strategically sensitive zone where the Middle East meets Europe. In over 20 years of post-Soviet independence, Azerbaijan has been a partner to the US and Europe in political and military areas and in energy. But it is not a democracy. The regime of Ilham Aliyev, which began with a tainted election in 2003, has moved away from even the limited democracy of his predecessor and father, Heydar Aliyev, former Communist Party First Secretary in the Soviet period. Under Ilham Aliyev's government, the authorities have increased repression of regime critics, opposition parties, youth movements, journalists and political bloggers, human rights defenders, NGOs and the lawyers who defend them against politically motivated charges. Fearing a color revolution or "EuroMaidan" threat, the Aliyev regime has greatly increased its repressions during 2014 and accused Western-led international organizations and the US in particular of subverting the Aliyev regime.

Geopolitical context: Begin with the map: Azerbaijan is the only country that borders both Iran and Russia, and must deal with various pressures arising from its location. As a former Soviet republic, and part of the Russian Empire before that since the early 19th century, it has close cultural, economic and political ties to Russia. With its primarily Muslim (mostly Shi'ite) population, and even earlier history as part of the Persian Empire, it has cultural bonds with Iran. These relationships are not simple. Russia is both a trade partner[1] and a threat. Iran dislikes Azerbaijan's secularism and relationship with Israel, and fears that Azerbaijan's Turkic national identity that may attract its own Azerbaijani population along their common border.

Like the entire South Caucasus, Azerbaijan is potentially in a pincer between events of Russia or Ukraine/Crimea and the Middle East. Iran has engaged with Baku most consistently, but in 2014-15, the ISIL threat has become urgent. Any government

---

[1] A new investment was agreed February 10, "Azerbaijan, Russia to sign plan for investment co-op until 2020," http://azeridaily.com/politics/4965

11

ruling Azerbaijan would have to deal with the pressures of the immediate neighbors and neighborhoods to the north (and northwest) and to the south (and southwest). If we consider also Azerbaijan's eastern neighbors across the Caspian in Central Asia, it becomes obvious that they figure in policies around energy, drugs, arms, human trafficking, terrorism, intelligence gathering and more.

As an energy-rich country, Azerbaijan benefits financially and its oil /gas output is strategically important to Europe and Turkey and potentially to other areas. Future gas supplies from Azerbaijan could, combined with gas from Iran, Iraq and Turkmenistan, provide substantial supplies through Turkey to southern Europe.

Azerbaijan is therefore an important country for US and European considerations of politics, energy, business investment, enforcement of laws against trafficking, and potentially as a bulwark against the increasing influence of Islamic extremism.

Independence and internal stability are fundamentals for economic and human development. No opposition group or individual within Azerbaijan has suggested that either independent statehood or internal stability should be abandoned. Critics oppose the regime, not the state. But the regime identifies itself with the state and claims that a threat to its own power is a threat to statehood. Under these conditions, endemic corruption, lack of democratic governance, and repression of critical voices undermine the stability of society and therefore put the country at risk. Partnership with such repressive leaders taints the US reputation - this has already happened in Azerbaijan. US support for undemocratic regimes puts the US at a disadvantage in its efforts - in Azerbaijan and around the world-- to promote democracy, civil society, human rights, in short, all the "self-evident" truths about human dignity and equality that we claim as the foundation of our system. This loss of prestige hurts US "soft power" in the world.

Human Rights and Democracy: For most of its post-Soviet existence, Azerbaijan rulers have been less than fully tolerant of views that disagree with them, their policies or the ruling party. Opposition parties, their members, their publications and on-line presence have been progressively constrained in various ways including economic discrimination, closing of offices, restricting of space for public meetings, arrests and legal action on bogus charges and other prosecution. The pressure on opposition groups and critics, especially youth, both in and outside political parties, and on NGOs has gradually increased since the 2003 accession to the presidency of Ilham Aliyev, son of the previous president and former Communist Party First Secretary and KGB general Heydar Aliyev. Since early 2013 the instances of such repressions have increased in number and intensity reaching unprecedented levels since the spring of 2014.[2]

Because 2013 was a presidential election year in Azerbaijan and because the incumbent was running for a controversial[3] 3rd term, the regime and the ruling party YAP (Yeni [New] Azerbaijan Party) raised the levels of criticism and repressions against opposition parties, especially the two major parties the Yeni Musavat and the Azerbaijan Popular Front Party (AXCP), but also the newly founded Republic Alternative known as REAL. During the campaign, members of Musavat and AXCP were harassed by police, detained for questioning, released, detained again, and sometimes subsequently arrested on bogus charges. The leader of REAL, Ilqar Mammedov, was arrested and remains in jail.

The Aliyev regime has targeted the generation in their 20s and 30s, especially men. Fearing the participation of this age group in the "color" revolutions in Ukraine and neighboring Georgia, then the Arab Spring of 2011, and in 2014, the "Maidan" protest movement in Ukraine, Azerbaijani authorities have targeted and arrested more young people and have charged them with more serious crimes than in previous years. The authorities began to incriminate political critics by planting drugs on the suspect's

---

[2] Summary in the HRW Report for 2015: http://www.hrw.org/world-report/2015/country-chapters/azerbaijan?page=1

[3] Opposition critics challenged the legality of the National Assembly's vote to remove term limitations to enable Aliyev to run for a third term. Rebecca Vincent, "Five Things Aliyev Doesn't want you to know about Azerbaijan's presidential elections." http://www.indexoncensorship.org/2013/10/five-things-aliyev-doesnt-want-know-azerbaijans-presidential-election/

person or in his car or home.[4] The accused was then arrested on drug charges rather than political ones.

Using these criminal charges, Azerbaijani authorities insist there are no political prisoners because those incarcerated are "criminals." Human Rights Watch (HRW) noted this pattern: *"The Azerbaijani authorities used a range of spurious narcotics and weapons possession, hooliganism, incitement, and even treason charges in 2013 to prosecute at least 23 political activists, journalists, bloggers, and human rights defenders critical of the government. All 23 are behind bars, most in pretrial custody."*[5]

The case of REAL leader Ilqar Mammedov exemplifies repression of both regime critics and the youth opposition since REAL's membership is largely under 40. Its founder Ilqar Mammedov was arrested in early 2013 on charges of instigating public unrest that had begun before his arrival in the town (Ismayilli) where it took place. During the early months of his incarceration, his followers in REAL collected the required 40,000 signatures for candidacy in the presidential election. But the Central Election Commission (CEC), dominated by the ruling party YAP, declared many to be forgeries and Mammedov was therefore not registered as a candidate. He was subsequently sentenced to seven years in prison. In May 2014, the European Court of Human Rights issued a judgment in the Mammedov case and found his arrest to be unlawful and a violation of legal processes and of the complainant's rights as guaranteed by the European Convention of Human Rights.[6] Nonetheless, and despite international protests, he remains in prison today.

"The Crackdown" During 2014, harassment, arrests and reports of physical abuse in custody increased to such a degree that it is widely referred to as "The Crackdown." The pattern of arrest for questioning, release, re-arrest was increasingly a prelude to

---

[4] Presidential contender and member of AXCP Jamil Hasanli noted this pattern in a television interview

[5] http://www.hrw.org/news/2014/01/21/azerbaijan-election-amid-rights-crackdown

[6] Kavkaz [Caucasian Knot} http://eng.kavkaz-uzel.ru/articles/28276/ and Amnesty International report: http://www.amnesty.org/en/news/azerbaijan-political-activists-held-fabricated-charges-must-be-released-2014-03-14; French government "deplores" sentence: http://www.diplomatie.gouv.fr/en/country-files/azerbaijan/events-7746/article/azerbaijan-sentencing-of-ilgar

arrest and detention. High-profile trials of youth activists resulted in long sentences. Six activists in the youth organization NIDA, who had been arrest in spring 2013, were sentenced in May 2014 to 6-8 years in prison.[7]

During July and August, arrests of human rights defenders and other critics reached a level of nearly one per week. Human Rights defender Leyla Yunus and her husband Arif Yunus, historian, were questioned and released in April, but arrested and charged with tax evasion, treason (for Track II diplomacy efforts) and other changes on July 30 and August 5, respectively. On August 8, head of the Human Rights Club Rasul Jafarov was arrested; he and Leyla had worked to create a unified list of political prisoners in Azerbaijan and now both were added to it. President Aliyev had stated in a NATO visit earlier in the year that Azerbaijan has no political prisoners. A week after Jafarov's arrest, human rights lawyer Intiqam Aliyev was arrested. In September opposition journalist Seymur Hazi was arrested on a charge of hooliganism. All remain in jail.

Treatment in custody has been poor, and defendants are regularly deprived of council. Requests for medicine by the Yunus couple and Intiqam Aliyev who are all in poor health, have been ignored. Charges by Leyla Yunus that she has been beaten have been dismissed by prison authorities as "lies of her lawyers." Several of her lawyers were declared to be witnesses against her and thus removed from her defense team. Later in the year another defense attorney Khalid Baghirov, associated with REAL and defender of Ilqar Mammedov, Leyla Yunus and others, was suspended and risks being disbarred.

The space for civil society activities has been increasingly constricted. Obstacles have been created since 2013 on NGOs so that registration is extremely difficult, acceptance of foreign grants –which was officially discouraged—is now almost impossible. NGOs in general are treated as instruments of foreign influence rather than vehicles for the initiatives and interests of Azerbaijani citizens. In 2014, bank

---

[7] Sources on NIDA: https://campaigns.amnesty.org/actions/youth-activists-Azerbaijan
http://www.hrw.org/news/2013/04/02/azerbaijan-authorities-targeting-youth-activists and (against their arrest and torture in 2013); and on sentences, Meydan TV: http://www.meydan.tv/en/site/news/1581/NIDA-Activists-Sentenced-%28UPDATED%29.htm

accounts of numerous NGOs including Oxfam, IREX (International Research and Exchanges Board), Transparency Azerbaijan (arm of Transparency International), loca partners of the Extractive Industries Transparency Initiative (EITI) and many of their CEOs were frozen forcing most to reduce activity or close their offices.

By December, many major NGOs were closed or had suspended activities. The number of political prisoners was over 100 – more than Russia and Belorus combined. Journalists were under increasing pressure, and the number of journalists in jail had doubled since the start of 2014, from about 8 to 15. In December one of the most prominent investigative journalists, Khadija Ismailova, was arrested on bogus charges. Although her accuser reportedly dropped charges, she was not only held, but her pre-trial detention was renewed for two more months. In late December, the Baku office of Radio Liberty, an independent but US funded media organization was raided and closed. Several prominent defense lawyers were being suspended or disbarred.[8]

Why now?

Ilham Aliyev came to power in 2003 and therefore had a front seat to the Georgian and Ukrainian "color" revolutions both of which involved tainted elections and activist youth. He surely paid attention to the Arab Spring of 2011. The 2013-14 crisis in Ukraine, the EuroMaidan in Kyiv was a case of a former Soviet republic trying to choose a path, perhaps strike a balance, between the West and Russia. Ukraine's elections were falsified and a substantial youth movement worked against the corrupt regime. Azerbaijan is not a simple analogy to Ukraine, but Aliyev's regime may well have been afraid of a public reaction against their rule, especially after the abuses of his own presidential campaign in October 2013 and the pressures against youth activists, opposition parties, and the media.

The Aliyev regime had already been positioning itself to quash dissent and stave off criticism with an array of "carrots and sticks":

---

[8] Khadija Ismailova's attorney is case in point; Giorgi Lomsadze "Azerbaijan: Next they come for the Lawyers?" http://www.eurasianet.org/node/71301

(1) Improve Azerbaijan's image abroad with such things as the beautification of Baku; invitations to foreign observers and businessmen; welcome foreign investment and ramp up sales of oil/gas; cultivate relations with European political organizations that do not monitor elections such as the Council of Europe (CoE) and host European cultural and sporting events. Regime victories here including Eurovision Song Competition in 2012, planned Euro Games for 2015, Formula One auto racing in 2016;

(2) preempt critics and watch dog group members with "caviar diplomacy," a short hand for legal lobbying as well as illegal vote buying, bribery, etc.[9] Their great victory of this policy was the rejection by the CoE of its own committee's report on political prisoners, Jan/Feb 2013.

(3) marginalize or exclude organizations that monitor elections such as OSCE/ODIHR (the OSCO office in Baku was downgraded in December 2013 to a projects office) and the domestic Election Monitoring and Democracy Studies Center whose head Anar Mammadli was arrest at the same time;

(4) quash internal dissent vigorously by targeting public demonstrations, opposition parties, media, NGOs and their finances and their leadership, all under the rubric of maintaining domestic order and stability and independence. Groups with outside funding or affiliations were vilified as "foreign agents" aiming to subvert Azerbaijan. This policy constituted a pre-emptive strike against opponents of the regime, not of threats to the Azerbaijani state.

Western Assessment: Andrew Stroehlein, Human Rights Watch (HRW) European Media Director noted the "Azerbaijani government's 'horrific crackdown' on civil society and critics, marking a dramatic deterioration in its already poor rights record. The HRW report says Azerbaijani authorities convicted or imprisoned at least 33 human rights defenders, political and civil activists, journalists, and bloggers on politically

---

[9] European Stability Initiative (ESI) report, 2012, "Caviar Diplomacy: How Azerbaijan Silenced the Council of Europe," http://www.esiweb.org/pdf/esi_document_id_131.pdf

motivated charges, while many independent civic groups were forced to cease their activities."[10]

In September 2014, the European Parliament adopted a resolution recognizing the worsening of the human rights situation over the previous five years. The UN Subcommittee on Human Rights cut short a visit to Azerbaijan because it was barred from visiting "places of detention" to which it had been promised access.[11] Wrote Nils Muiznieks, Council of Europe Commissioner for Human Rights, after his visit in October 2014 to Azerbaijan: *"Azerbaijan will go down in history as the country that carried out an unprecedented crackdown on human rights defenders during its chairmanship [of the CoE Committee of Ministers]. All of my partners in Azerbaijan are in jail."*[12]

Targeting the US: Criticism of the OSCE, the EU, and other international organizations has become a staple of Aliyev regime rhetoric. But the overt and sharp accusations against the US spiked in 2014 seemingly an echo of Russian accusations about the US as instigator of the Kyiev Maidan.[13] Official statements from Baku raised the specter of US instigation at every color revolution, the Arab Spring, Ukraine's EuroMaidan, and the rise of ISIL. A long, vitriolic, and tendentious article by presidential chief of staff Ramiz Mehtiyev appeared in December 3, 2014.[14] Mehtiyev argued NGOs represent "foreign interests" trying to destabilize Azerbaijan. Mehtiyev went so far as to accuse the West and the US specifically[15] of attempting to subvert Azerbaijan in the guise of democracy building and of using Azerbaijani citizens and

---

[10] ww.rferl.org/content/human-rights-watch-report-2015-russia-ukraine-iraq-azerbaijan/26819455.html

[11] http://www.ohchr.org/EN/NewsEvents/Pages/DisplayNews.aspx?NewsID=15047&LangID=E

[12] "Nils Muiznieks: Azerbaijan's reprisals against brave activists and journalists must stop now," posted November 24 http://www.indexoncensorship.org/2014/11/nils-muiznieks-azerbaijans-reprisals-brave-activists-journalists-must-stop-now/

[13] http://azeridaily.com/news/4953

[14] Ramiz Mehtiyev, "Ikili standartlarin dunya nizami ve muasir Azerbaican," posted 3 December 2014, http://news.milli.azpolitics/312011.html

[15] He named European Union President Martin Schultz and US President Barak Obama, accusing them of political ignorance and trying to overthrow the Aliyev regime in the guise of building democracy using NGOs.

NGOs as a "fifth column." The message to the domestic audience is that working for an NGO is subversive and reflects disloyalty. By extension, criticism of regime policies is treason. This tirade against the West and Western values led one analyst, a former US ambassador to Azerbaijan, to argue that the regime's position "undoes two decades" of relationship-building between Azerbaijan and the US.[16]

The anti-American posture was not merely in the rhetoric. Last September, in detaining Said Nuri, a US citizen of Azerbaijani origin, the Prosecutor's office stated it "does not recognize" his US citizenship.[17] After several weeks he was released and allowed to return to the US. The arrest of Khadija Ismailova has created a far greater international stir. She was arrested two days after she was named in Ramiz Mehtiyev's article as being "disloyal" to Azerbaijan because she works for Radio Liberty. She remains in jail today. In late December, Azerbaijani authorities raided the local RL office, *Azadliq Radiosu*, taking all the staff for questioning (including the cleaning woman), seizing computers, and sealing the offices. The staff was later questioned again, without an attorney, some in the middle of the night in their pajamas.[18]

The US State Department adjusted its tone from gently reminding Azerbaijan of its international obligations in June of last year[19] to calling for an end to restrictions on civil society in August when the US representative to the OSCE released a statement identifying individuals arrested on politically motivated charges and calling on the government of Azerbaijan to release its political prisoners.[20] By year's end, State

---

[16] Richard D. Kauzlarich, "The Heydar Aliyev Era Ends in Azerbaijan Not with a Bang but a Whisper," posted January 13, 2015,
http://www.brookings.edu/research/opinions/2015/01/13-aliyev-era-ends-bang-whisper-azerbaijan-kauzlarich
[17] RFE/RL Azerbaijani service, September 4, 2014, http://www.azadliq.org/content/article/26565995.html
[18] Among detailed international coverage of this incident and its aftermath are these:
http://www.rferl.org/content/azerbaijan-rferl-baku-bureau-raided/26763449.html,
http://www.japantimes.co.jp/news/2014/12/29/world/detained-radio-liberty-journalists-questioned-azerbaijan/#.VNpfoC7PosQ, http://en.rsf.org/azerbaidjan-rfe-rl-s-baku-bureau-falls-victim-26-12-2014,47427.html
[19] Testimony of Deputy Assistant Secretary of State Thomas O. Melia to the Helsinki Commission, June 11, 2014, http://www.state.gov/j/drl/rls/rm/2014/227450.htm; State Dept statement of October
http://www.state.gov/r/pa/prs/ps/2014/10/233268.htm;
[20] http://photos.state.gov/libraries/azerbaijan/749085/highlights/osce_Azerbaijan_Ongoing_Detentions.pdf

Department spokesperson Jan Psaki expressed concern that Azerbaijan is not living up to its international commitments in human rights.[21]

Room for Engagement?

The year 2015 will be pivotal for the coming 5 years in Azerbaijan and in US-Azerbaijani relations. Azerbaijan must maintain friendly relations with its neighbors and commercial partners. Recent signs suggest that the regime, or at least some people among the power elite, are trying to bring the country closer Russia in foreign policy and in the handling of domestic criticism. Despite Aliyev's visits to Putin and the rhetoric of friendship, there is a limit to that shift. Ilham Aliyev and most of his inner circle want to be seen as Western and get the business deals and the life-style benefits the West has to offer. It is more likely that Azerbaijani leaders will seek a new balance among its neighbors and principal partners, Russia, Iran, Israel, Turkey, and the West including the US.

Fearing for its survival, the regime is likely to maintain its clamp-down on civil society. This is not only anti-democratic, but also a risky and counter-productive strategy for the regime itself. Polls show the population as a whole is most immediately concerned with pocket book issues. This is not good news for the regime with falling oil prices that reduce state revenue. Lower revenues will lead to spending cuts and thus fewer jobs. Pensions and state salaries are already low and would not be raised. The same pattern of joblessness in Russia could send home hundreds of thousands of migrant workers who return to see poverty in their native village compared to the luxuries and lavish spending by the ruling elites. Many historical examples show that without official governance mechanisms for the redress of grievances or civil society space for discussion of problems and debate over solutions, people turn to radical actions and sometimes also to radical leaders. Demonstrations become likely and if the police crack down on them, people will become more belligerent and a "BakuMaidan" can begin.

---

[21] http://www.state.gov/r/pa/prs/dpb/2014/12/234568.htm#AZERBAIJAN

The US can plan an important role in aiding Azerbaijan. First and foremost, the United States and its representatives must be unapologetic about our commitment to human rights and democracy. The US owes this much to the pro-democracy movements and groups in Azerbaijan. The US has lost respect and credibility among the population by its support for the Aliyev regime and its repressive policies. Only by difficult negotiations might the US persuade this regime of the need for reform that would benefit the Azerbaijani people and improve its own standing in the world.

-END-

Biographical note: Dr. Audrey L. Altstadt is Professor of History at the University of Massachusetts, Amherst and during 2014-15, a Fellow at the Woodrow Wilson International Center for Scholars in Washington DC.

Mr. ROHRABACHER. Well, thank you, Doctor.
And Dr. Cornell?

STATEMENT OF SVANTE CORNELL, PH.D., DIRECTOR, CENTRAL ASIA–CAUCASUS INSTITUTE, SCHOOL OF ADVANCED INTERNATIONAL STUDIES, JOHNS HOPKINS UNIVERSITY

Mr. CORNELL. Thank you, Mr. Chairman. I have a longer written testimony for the record, and I will be summarizing some of the points here.

I will start by saying that the U.S. relationship to Azerbaijan was once a well-functioning strategic partnership. Today it is dominated by tension and acrimony. In the next minutes, I will try to provide my perspective on why this is the case but, more importantly, what we can do about it.

Mr. ROHRABACHER. Doctor, could you hold on for one moment?

Mr. CORNELL. Sure.

Mr. ROHRABACHER. Is that a vote? Are those votes? No?

You know, I have been here all these years; I can't figure out those lights yet. [Laughter.]

Recess? All right, good.

All right, you may proceed.

Mr. CORNELL. Thank you, sir.

To start with, I would like to say a few words about why Azerbaijan in this region matters to the U.S. Several of the members here have mentioned these things.

I will start by saying that, in a 1997 book, former National Security Advisor Zbigniew Brzezinski called Azerbaijan one of the five geopolitical pivot countries of Eurasia. Azerbaijan lies at the intersection of the key Eurasian powers, Russia, Iran, and Turkey. It is a bottleneck of the east-west corridor that connects Europe to Central Asia and beyond for the purposes of trade, for energy, but also for U.S. military access, as in Afghanistan.

And I would say that in the present situation, where the two most acute challenges to the Trans-Atlantic Alliance are Russia's aggressive expansionism as well as Islamic radicalism emanating from the Middle East, Azerbaijan and its neighbors are actually a bulwark against both. There is, indeed, an opportunity in the existence of Muslim majority states that reject Russian projects of coerced Eurasian integration, maintain the openness of the east-west corridor into Central Asia, and remain committed to secular statehood. And, of course, this is all the more crucial, given Iran's continued jockeying for regional domination from Syria to Yemen and Turkey's turn toward an Islamism and anti-Western authoritarianism.

This is not just a theoretical point. Looking back to 9/11, America's military response in Central Asia was made possible by the air corridor across Georgia and Azerbaijan, which you, Mr. Chairman, correctly characterized as irreplaceable.

Now for most of the past decade, the broader regional picture is that America's ability to affect the developments in Azerbaijan and the entire region has been in decline. I would even say that at no time since the collapse of the Soviet Union has the U.S. had less influence over regional matters than it does today.

Now this is the context, of course, of the discussion we are having today, and it is customary to blame the Azerbaijani domestic evolution for the decline of the U.S.-Azerbaijani bilateral relationship. That is, indeed, a factor. But, a decade ago, it is important to note that the Azerbaijani Government was considerably more responsive to U.S. criticism and advice on its domestic affairs.

So, the question is, what has changed in the past decade and why is it not today? Now the most obvious point has been already made, which is that oil and gas has brought wealth to Azerbaijan. Twenty years ago it was a failing state. Today it is wealthy. There is a growing reluctance to take advice from abroad.

A more important factor, I would argue, is the worsening regional security environment. Only in the past few years, Russia has invaded Georgia, invaded Ukraine, contributed to orchestrating a coup in Kyrgyzstan, and forced Armenia to abstain from any form of European integration.

Russian subversion is on the rise everywhere in the region, and the case of Azerbaijan there are also growing tendencies not only by Iran, but also by Turkey, of meddling in internal affairs. And all of this has grown a powerful inhibition liberalization.

Unfortunately, I would say that U.S. policies have actually been an important contributing factor to this situation. In fact, for the past 20 years, the U.S. relationship with Azerbaijan was built on the understanding that the U.S. has interests in several diverse areas, which you have mentioned and which are in the title of this hearing.

Human rights and democracy was one area. The second was engagement on energy issues, and the third, of course, was cooperation on security affairs, including America's role in negotiating a solution to the Armenian and Azerbaijan conflict.

If you will, these three areas formed a tripod that was the basis of U.S. policy, and the problem is that this tripod has faltered, because American engagement in energy issues and security issues over the past decade have declined, I would say, drastically. Now I want to be clear here. My argument is not that the U.S. has engaged too deeply in democracy promotion. The problem is that the U.S. has not provided enough attention to security——

Mr. ROHRABACHER. Is your microphone on?

Mr. CORNELL. I believe so.

So, I want to be clear that my argument is not that the U.S. has engaged too deeply in democracy promotion. The problem is that it has not provided enough attention to security issues and energy issues. And the important fact is that these were the issues that provided America with leverage in Azerbaijan.

Now the U.S. also made a number of missteps after the Russian invasion of Georgia. I could discuss these in detail, including how the Russian Reset was handled, the fact that the Turkish-Armenian normalization process was prioritized over the Nagorno-Karabakh conflict, all of which alienated Azerbaijan and reduced the value of the U.S. for its national interests.

Now the U.S. has also not properly understood, I would say, the effect of inter-regime politics in Azerbaijan in this, and Dr. Altstadt alluded to that. As the current policy is not working, what can be done looking forward?

My Institute has newly released a paper on Western Strategy in the South Caucuses, which I am sure your staff will be made available, in which we propose a detailed outline of what a new U.S. strategy toward the region would look like.

Now some have argued for a tougher approach; that is, a policy that would include punitive measures. Of course, that would, first of all, amount of singling out Azerbaijan since the U.S. does not apply such policies for countries that have worse human rights records, and it would also be counterproductive in a country where compact frustration which they see as the American indifference to the hundreds of thousands of displaced people from the Karabakh conflict.

More importantly, such an approach would also be certain to fail. Since the ruling elite presently does not see much of a meaningful U.S. involvement in key matters of national security, the U.S. today simply does not have the leverage to influence Baku's policies by the use of the proverbial stick. Instead, I feel that such steps would extinguish whatever influence the U.S. still has in the country.

Instead, what I would call for and what we call for in our paper is a broad strategic re-engagement, not only of Azerbaijan, but of the entire region. I would say that in the past 20 years, whenever the U.S. has been strongly involved in the security issues and the energy issues of this region, the Azerbaijani Government has actually been responsive to criticism. When that has not been the case, like now, America's leverage has declined. So, going forward, I would say that the U.S. cannot expect realistically to see any progress in governance and human rights issues without a clear engagement on the issues of security and energy.

Similarly, I think Azerbaijan's leaders should understand that they cannot expect U.S. support on security issues and energy issues without a commitment to reforms in governance and human rights. Again, this does not mean that a new policy should have less of an emphasis on human rights issues, but it does mean that the U.S. must engage the government on a broader front and do more to address the issues on which it worked effectively a decade ago. These are bolstering sovereignty and independence, addressing security issues, working seriously, which we have not done, to resolve the Armenian-Azerbaijan conflict, and re-engaging on energy politics. All of these also happen to be in the U.S. national interest.

So, in closing, for both Azerbaijan's domestic situation and our bilateral relationship to improve, America's presence must once again be felt in the region, which it is not today.

Thank you.

[The prepared statement of Mr. Cornell follows:]

"Azerbaijan: U.S. Energy, Security, and Human Rights Interests"

Testimony of Dr. Svante E. Cornell
Director, Central Asia-Caucasus Institute
School of Advanced International Studies
The Johns Hopkins University

Given before the United States House of Representatives
Committee on Foreign Affairs
Subcommittee on Europe, Eurasia and Emerging Threats

February 12, 2015

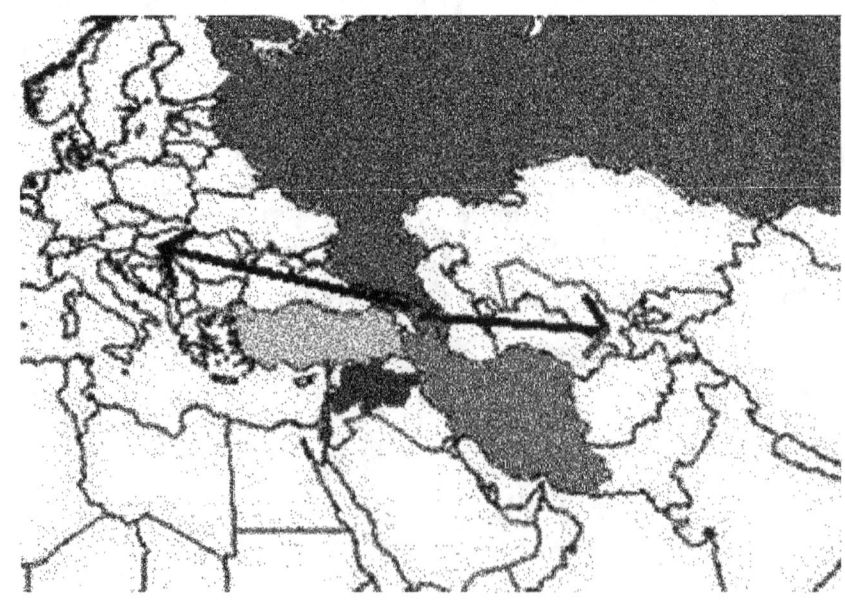

Introduction[1]

This hearing occurs at a low point in relations between Azerbaijan and the United States, a relationship that was once a well-functioning strategic partnership characterized by a high level of trust. To understand the reasons behind this state of affairs, and especially to seek ways to improve the current situation, it is necessary to briefly delve into Azerbaijan's regional security situation and its politics; and not least, the policy of the U.S. in Eastern Europe and Eurasia more broadly.

Azerbaijan's situation has unique characteristics, but the topic today is part and parcel of several larger trends: first of all, it is an acute case of the declining influence of the West, and particularly the United States, in all of post-communist Europe and Eurasia – in all sectors, including security, energy and human rights. Secondly, the decline of Azerbaijan's relationship with the U.S. bears similarities to tensions in America's ties with a number of other allies, from Israel to South Korea, that have grown wary of U.S. foreign policy.

Before delving into these matters, it is important to review briefly why Azerbaijan and its region matters to America's interests.

Why Does Azerbaijan Matter, and What Are U.S. Interests?

The main importance of Azerbaijan and the Caucasus lies in its crucial geographical location at the intersection of multiple crossroads. It lies between the Black and Caspian seas, and thus between Europe and Asia as well as providing the land link between Russia and the Middle East. Its key strategic value is twofold. On one hand, it lies at the intersection between Russia, Iran and Turkey, powers playing key roles in international politics. On the other, it is the bottleneck of the burgeoning east-west corridor connecting Europe to Central Asia and beyond. In this Caucasus corridor, Azerbaijan is the only country bordering both Russia and Iran, and therefore the geopolitically most pivotal country. Former National Security Advisor Zbigniew Brzezinski acknowledged this in his 1997 book *The Grand Chessboard*, in which he termed Azerbaijan one of the five geopolitical pivots of Eurasia together with Ukraine, South Korea, Turkey and Iran.

As a result, Azerbaijan and its region is key to western efforts to shape the future of the intersection of Europe and the Middle East, and to any reaction to crises occurring in this wider area. It also plays a central role in western access to the heart of the Eurasian continent, whether it be for energy, transport, trade, or military purposes.

The strategic importance of Azerbaijan and its region can also be stated in terms of the current difficult moment in international politics, where the two most salient challenges to the transatlantic alliance are Russia's aggressive expansionism, and the Islamic radicalism emanating from the Middle East.

The states of the Caucasus and Central Asia, Azerbaijan in particular, are unique as they are an important pressure point in *both* directions. The task of countering Putin's Russian imperialism goes beyond Ukraine, and requires a firm strategy to bolster the states on Russia's periphery, and especially to maintain the crucial east-west corridor to Central Asia open. But the Caucasus and Central Asia also include fully one half of secular Muslim-majority states in the world. These states

---

[1] This testimony builds on the publication "A Western Strategy for the South Caucasus", authored by Svante E. Cornell, S. Frederick Starr, and Mamuka Tsereteli, released in February 2015 and available at http://www.silkroadstudies.org/publications/silkroad-papers-and-monographs/item/13075.

may have far to go in terms of democratic development, but their governments and populations are committed to the separation of state and religion, to secular laws, and to the protection of state and society from religious extremism. Azerbaijan is unique in being a majority Shi'a Muslim state, bordering Iran, which is based on a secular form of statehood.

Thus, the Caucasus (and Central Asia) should be seen as bulwarks against both Moscow and the Islamic radicalism of the Middle East. This is amplified by other regional trends. The Iranian theocracy continues to assertively expand its regional influence, as events from Syria to Iraq to Yemen indicate. In Turkey, the deterioration of secular government has given rise to a growing anti-western authoritarianism with Islamist underpinnings, endangering the Turkish-American alliance. As a country sharing linguistic bonds with Turkey and religious ties with Iran, Azerbaijan is once again uniquely situated.

As mentioned, Azerbaijan is the lynchpin in the land bridge that the Caucasus constitutes linking Europe with Central Asia. This is important concretely in terms both of Europe's energy security, and America's military access to the heart of Eurasia, including Afghanistan.

The creation of a pipeline system connecting Azerbaijan's Caspian Sea oil and gas resources via Turkey to Europe, which began a decade ago, broke the Russian monopoly over the exportation of Caspian energy resources, and provides Europe with an important source of diversification. Through Azerbaijan, Europe has the opportunity to access Central Asia's even larger natural gas resources.

Second, after the terrorist attacks of September 11, 2001, the U.S. faced the enormous challenge of waging a war in the heart of the Eurasian continent, thousands of miles from the closest U.S. military base. America's response was made possible by the introduction of U.S. military power into Central Asia – which was achieved in turn through the air corridor across Georgia and Azerbaijan. Later, a Northern Distribution Network was created which includes access through Russia; but given the state of Russia-West relations, that corridor cannot be counted on. Moscow has already on two occasions in the past few months blocked the German Air Force from using Russian territory to supply its presence in Afghanistan. Thus, access through Azerbaijan will remain crucial for any continued presence in Afghanistan or future contingencies.

In sum, therefore, the Caucasus and particularly Azerbaijan has an important place in the western strategy to meet imminent threats in Eastern Europe and the Middle East, as well as in long-term contingencies for a variety of challenges in the wider region. The U.S. has a serious and strategic interest in ensuring that the Caucasus, and Azerbaijan, maintain a positive relationship with the West, and remain open for western access.

Concrete U.S. Interests

The title of this hearing correctly assumes that the relations between Azerbaijan and the United States occur in diverse areas, usually summarized as security, energy and human rights; and that the U.S. has important interests in each area. In more specific and concrete terms, American interests in Azerbaijan and the region can be summarized as follows:

- For Azerbaijan and the states of the Caucasus to be stable, sovereign and self-governing states controlled by none of their neighboring powers; and cooperating actively with Western governments and institutions on regional security, counter-terrorism and conflict resolution.

- For the conflicts of the Caucasus, particularly the Armenian-Azerbaijani conflict, to be placed on a path toward long-term and peaceful resolution, within the framework of international law, and with the degree of manipulation of external powers minimized.
- For Azerbaijan to be a state with secular laws in a geographical environment that includes theocratic Iran, Iraq, the North Caucasus, and Turkey.
- For Azerbaijan and its neighbors to evolve gradually but assuredly into a zone of self-governing, law-based states that respect human rights, are free of corruption, and are responsive to citizens' needs.
- For Azerbaijan and its neighbors to be a source and transit corridor for energy, in particular contributing to diversifying the sources of Europe's energy supplies, and to function as a reliable territory for Western access by land and air to and from Central and South Asia.
- For Azerbaijan and its neighbors to develop into an important land trade corridor connecting Europe, China, and India not controlled by any of them but protected by all.

Unfortunately, developments over the past decade have not furthered these interests. The sovereignty of the regional states is increasingly under question as blatant interference by Russia has mounted, complemented by lesser degrees of meddling by Iran and Turkey. The Armenian-Azerbaijani conflict is on a path of escalation, not resolution. Azerbaijan remains committed to secular laws, but the political development of the country and its rights record has come under increasingly strong criticism. The development of the energy corridor to the West has been stalled and faced multiple hurdles in the past decade. Progress toward making the Caucasus a land corridor is proceeding, but at a slow speed.

Meanwhile, for most of the past decade, America's ability to affect developments in Azerbaijan and the entire region has been in decline. In retrospect, the 2008 Russian invasion of Georgia was a turning point, after which the situation in the region, and western influence there, has deteriorated. In fact, it is no exaggeration to state that at no time since the collapse of the Soviet Union has the U.S. had less influence over regional matters than today.

Changes in the Region: Impact on the U.S.-Azerbaijan Relationship

The U.S.-Azerbaijan relationship is the most acute exhibit of a trend of declining American influence. A decade ago, this was a relatively strong strategic partnership, characterized by mutual respect and a functioning dialogue between two governments. Today, its main characteristic is bitter acrimony on both sides.

What are the reasons for this? It is customary to blame Azerbaijan's domestic evolution for the decline in the relationship. While this is one factor, the question that should be asked is how the U.S. could have allowed a relationship with a geostrategic pivot country like Azerbaijan to deteriorate so badly, and without taking serious and visible efforts to engage its leadership until very recently. A decade ago, the Azerbaijani government was considerably more responsive to U.S. criticism and advice concerning its domestic political system, management of elections, and human rights record. What has changed in the past decade, and why is this no longer the case?

First, Azerbaijan has benefited from a large inflow of wealth from its oil and gas industry. It was the fastest-growing economy in the world for several years – a major change in a country that was in a dilapidated condition, indeed a failing state, only twenty years ago. That has brought an ability to provide adequate funding to state institutions; co-opt large portions of the elite, particularly young professionals; as well as acquire legitimacy in considerable chunks of society. Opinion polling from the respected Caucasus Research Resource Centers shows that the broader population's approval of government services is growing, not falling. This new-found wealth has led to a growing reluctance to take advice from abroad; this factor has been compounded by the intra-elite politics within the government, as discussed below.

A more important factor is the regional environment, which has worsened considerably. Aggressive Russian efforts to reassert control over the former Soviet republics have contributed to a siege mentality. In the past seven years, Russia has invaded two post-Soviet states (Georgia and Ukraine) militarily, helped orchestrate a coup d'état in a third (Kyrgyzstan), and strong-armed a fourth (Armenia) to drop all efforts at European integration in favor of the Eurasian Union. Russian subversion is on the rise across the former Soviet sphere, as it is in western countries. To this should be added constant Iranian subversive activities, as well as a growing tendency by Turkey to interfere in Azerbaijan's internal affairs. This, put together, has formed a powerful inhibitor against loosening government control over state and society.

Missteps in American Policies

However, U.S. policies – or the lack thereof – have been an important contributing factor. It is important to recall that America's relationship with Azerbaijan, like all former Soviet states, was built on several components. A constructive dialogue on human rights and democracy was one of these. Another was American engagement in supporting the development of the east-west energy corridor, which enabled Azerbaijan to market is resources independently. A third was close cooperation on security issues, which included America's efforts to help resolve the Armenian-Azerbaijani conflict, as well as bilateral cooperation on defense, security, intelligence sharing and counter-terrorism.

These three areas, then, formed a tripod upon which U.S. policy was based. But in the past decade, that tripod has for all practical purposes faltered. American engagement in energy issues was strong down to the completion of initial pipeline infrastructure ten years ago; it has declined since then. The position of a U.S. Special Envoy for Eurasian Energy has been abolished; and America's role in the efforts to bring Caspian natural gas to Europe is minimal. Security interests gained salience after 9/11, but began a slow decline after 2003 as U.S. attention shifted to Iraq and European governments were unwilling to pick up the slack. Not least, U.S. leadership in resolving the Armenian-Azerbaijani conflict has been missing.

As a result, for most practical purposes, the promotion of democracy and human rights has been the only leg of U.S. policy proceeding at full speed, leading to an imbalance in the tripod that forms the underpinning of American strategy. Furthermore, this is certainly the way the relationship is seen from Baku's perspective. In large parts of the elite, this has led to a growing questioning of U.S. motivations, and a growing inclination to entertain conspiracy theories (propagated not least by Russian media) on alleged American plots to overthrow governments.

To be clear, the argument here is not that the U.S. has engaged too deeply in democracy promotion. The problem is that the U.S. has not balanced that important commitment with equal attention to security and energy, and has not adapted its methods to be successful in view of evolving regional realities.

In this context, the period following the 2008 war in Georgia was a watershed. That war laid bare the brute force Russia was willing to deploy to achieve its interests; it also showed that the West did not function as an effective deterrent against Russia. Not staying at that, the two American initiatives that most affected Azerbaijan were profoundly counter-productive for the bilateral relationship.

First, rather than causing Russia to pay a price for its invasion of an independent state, the Obama administration rewarded Moscow with the "Reset" initiative. U.S. officials claimed it would not come at the price of relations with smaller post-Soviet states; but in practice, it did. America's weak response to the invasion of Georgia, it should be said in retrospect, led the Kremlin to conclude it could get away with an even more brazen attack on Ukraine without lasting, serious consequences. In Baku, it led Azerbaijani leaders to question the rationale of the country's westward orientation.

Second, the Obama administration did not conclude from the Georgia war that it should spend additional efforts and energy on resolving the *other* unresolved conflict in the Caucasus – that between Armenia and Azerbaijan. Instead, it decided to embark on a project to normalize Turkish-Armenian relations. The core of that initiative was to open the Turkish-Armenian border, which Turkey had closed in 1993 because of Armenia's occupation of Azerbaijan's territory. Since that time, a link had been maintained between Turkish-Armenian relations and the Armenia-Azerbaijan conflict. The United States now pushed to cut that link, something that would heavily damage Azerbaijan's interests, without offering Baku anything in the process. This initiative effectively was understood in Baku to mean that Azerbaijan's most important national security issue was no longer an American concern. At roughly the same time, America's handling of the Arab upheavals, and its perceived endorsement of revolutions that brought Islamist forces to power, further exacerbated perceptions of American intentions.

Further, the U.S. has failed to draw the implications of Azerbaijan's complex and opaque internal political scene. Because the formal opposition is marginalized, American observers have generally assumed that President Aliyev exercises autocratic power. On this basis they pay little attention to intra-government politics. Yet Azerbaijan's internal politics are complex, and take place to a significant extent *within* the government rather than between government and opposition. Notwithstanding the formidable powers that the Constitution accords the President, his power are in reality far from complete.

In fact, in the 1990s, Azerbaijan's government developed a number of fiefdoms, the masters of which have shown an ability to effectively check the chief executive's powers. Internal rivalries exist in many countries, and can debilitate effective governance anywhere. But in Azerbaijan, two factors exacerbate them: first, these forces are strongest in the chief 'power institutions' of the state. Second, they have a thinly disguised (and in some cases overtly stated) affinity for Russia over the West, and maintain close ties to counterparts in Moscow that date back to the Soviet period. These forces have tended to oppose, and even undermine, Azerbaijan's relations with the West. While President Aliyev and his appointees have consistently sought to deepen Azerbaijan's relations with the West, resilient forces whose positions date back to before Aliyev came to power in 2003 have used their power to restrict civil society organizations and cracked down on dissidents at times that often appear chosen *specifically* to undermine the country's relations with the West.

Meanwhile, the U.S. has effectively linked improved bilateral relations in all areas with the advancement of democratic reforms and human rights. This is certainly laudable in principle. But in practice, in the absence of a solid American strategy toward the region, the implication has been to give the most anti-Western forces in the government a *de facto* veto over Azerbaijan's relations with the United States. This has benefited only the forces in the region seeking to diminish U.S. influence.

Put otherwise, American actions in response to deplorable restrictive regulations and instances of detention of dissidents have inadvertently reinforced the most retrograde elements in the government and contributed to isolating the very forces in the government that advocate for reform, and for integration with the West. By curtailing engagement in other areas of common interest, e.g. security and energy, American and European leaders have inadvertently alienated some of their closest potential partners in the region.

In the final analysis, the problem with U.S. policy has been, at the basic level, the absence of a concrete strategy that defines America's interests in the region, appreciates the existence of separate interests, while at all times taking into account the interactions between these areas of interest.

The Way Forward

Taking as a starting point that the U.S.-Azerbaijan relationship is important to the U.S. national interest, what can be done to improve it?

It is sometimes implied that Azerbaijan is building closer ties with Russia. In a sense, at least for the caricature of Azerbaijan prevalent in Western media, turning toward Moscow would seem to be a natural choice. But in fact, Azerbaijan is one of the former Soviet states that has been the most determined in resisting Russian efforts at Eurasian integration. Instead, Azerbaijan fundamentally remains oriented toward the West, even though that orientation is increasingly tenuous. Aside from pipeline infrastructure, the country is a member of the Council of Europe, and joined the European Union's Eastern Partnership in 2009. European identity remains an important element of Azerbaijan's self-image, as the country's eagerness to host the first European Games in 2015 shows. As Baku's relationship with the West has cooled, it has nevertheless moved gradually toward a position of non-alignment: while abstaining from deeper integration with Russia, Azerbaijan also eschews integration with Europe, attempting instead to "go it alone".

In view of the turbulence of its region, western missteps, and growing Russian pressure detailed above, what is remarkable is in fact how consistent Azerbaijan's foreign policy has been. In many ways, Azerbaijan's view of the United States is similar to that which can be found among numerous other American allies from Israel to South Korea and from Bahrain to Saudi Arabia: confusion bordering on disbelief over America's policies and intentions, and a sense of frustration and abandonment. In other words, it is indicative of a broader problem regarding America's place in the world.

That said, at this time of considerable turmoil both to Azerbaijan's north and south, the United States both can, and should, develop a new approach to Azerbaijan and its region, as the current policy is clearly not working. To this effect, several observers including former senior officials, have argued for an approach that is even tougher on Azerbaijan, including punitive measures. Yet such an approach would be sure to fail, because it presupposes a level of American leverage that is simply not in existence. In the current environment, a policy that would make U.S. policy even more one-dimensional would have almost no prospect of bringing positive results. The ruling elite does not perceive that it benefits from its association with the U.S. in key matters of national security;

therefore, the U.S. simply does not have the leverage it once had to influence Baku's policies by the use of the proverbial stick.

Furthermore, singling out Azerbaijan makes little sense in the absence of similar measures against regional countries with worse human rights records. Frustration with western indifference to the plight of the hundreds of thousands of displaced people from the Armenian-occupied territories in Mountainous Karabakh and western Azerbaijan is already high in Azerbaijan, and any further targeting of Azerbaijan would reinforce the sense of western double standards, which officials at very high levels already denounce.

In fact, given the prevailing frustration with the west and the character of the country's intra-elite politics, such steps would be likely to alienate Azerbaijan even further, and could in fact extinguish whatever influence the U.S. still commands in the country. The main victims of such an outcome would be not the ruling elite, but the proponents of human rights and democracy in Azerbaijan itself.

Instead, what is needed is a policy rooted in a regional strategy, which is based on a broad re-engagement of the region. A new American policy must coordinate and find the right balance and sequence among its priorities. In this context, a much stronger engagement in issues pertaining to sovereignty and security will do more than anything else to pave the way for progress in other areas, including human rights. The history of the past twenty years shows that whenever the U.S. has been strongly involved in energy and security affairs of the Caucasus, the Azerbaijani government has been responsive to criticism. When that has not been the case, as in the past several years, America's leverage has declined.

In short, going forward, the U.S. cannot expect progress on governance and human rights without a clear commitment to security issues; concomitantly, Azerbaijan's leaders must understand that they cannot expect Western support for their security without a commitment to reforms in governance and human rights. As already noted, this does not mean that a new policy should have less of an emphasis on human rights issues. But it means the U.S. must do more also to address the issues on which it worked effectively a decade ago: bolstering sovereignty and independence, addressing security issues, working seriously to resolve the Armenian-Azerbaijani conflict, and re-engaging on energy politics – all of which happen to be in U.S. national interest. In sum, for both Azerbaijan's domestic situation and the bilateral relationship to improve, America's presence must once again be felt in the region.

Mr. ROHRABACHER. Thank you very much.

And we have been joined, also, by Congressman Keating. Do you have an opening statement that you would like to make before our next witness?

Mr. KEATING. Thank you, Mr. Chairman. It is great to be back here with yourself and Ranking Member Meeks.

Like so many on the panel, I have had many discussions focused on Azerbaijan's strategic relevance and geopolitical importance. Its potential can't be underestimated. Yet, the potential alone of that cannot bear fruit in the global arena without adequate rule of law and basic protections and freedoms.

Unfortunately, we have seen a drastic regression in the rule of law, freedom of expression, freedom of assembly, transparency, and other basic rights in Azerbaijan. And I am particularly concerned over the deliberate targeting of American and international NGOs and media. These organizations that have been able to provide vital assistance to local citizens have already been forced to close. They include IREX, the National Democratic Institute, the International Republican Institute, the U.S. Peace Corps, Transparency International, and Oxfam.

Last month I spoke out in regard to the latest scapegoat of Azerbaijan authorities, Radio Free Europe. The government-sponsored raid on Baku Bureau and the arrest of and continued detention of Khadija Ismayilova, as well as others, raise serious questions and concerns over the intentions of the Azerbaijan leadership and the desire to partner with the U.S. and the West as a whole.

It should be noted that the regular conspiratorial pronouncements of Azeri officials against the U.S. and the West raise similar concerns. Yet, many of us who watch Azerbaijan continue to hope to see a change in the course of Azerbaijan. In this way, I urge the U.S. administration to prioritize these concerns when addressing Azerbaijan leadership. In particular, I hope that our Government will work to reopen Radio Free Europe in Baku and ensure a safe passage of Emin Heseynov, the husband of a U.S. Army servicewoman who spent the last 6 months sheltered in the Swiss Embassy in Baku.

Again, I thank you for holding this important hearing and look forward to working with you on this important issue, Mr. Chairman.

Mr. ROHRABACHER. Thank you very much.

Mr. KEATING. I yield back.

Mr. ROHRABACHER. And now, for our last witness, Mr. Kauzlarich, go right ahead. Or, Ambassador, I should say.

STATEMENT OF THE HONORABLE RICHARD KAUZLARICH, AD-JUNCT PROFESSOR, SCHOOL OF PUBLIC POLICY, GEORGE MASON UNIVERSITY (FORMER AMERICAN AMBASSADOR TO AZERBAIJAN)

Ambassador KAUZLARICH. Thank you, Mr. Chairman, and thank you and the committee for holding these hearings and giving me the opportunity to testify.

I have submitted a written statement for the record and, with your permission, I will summarize that statement now.

I agree with the previous speakers that we are at a critical point in U.S.-Azerbaijani relations, though I take a little more positive view of what we have accomplished in two decades of successful diplomatic engagement. This engagement has been based on a clear set of bipartisan objectives. Despite the restrictions of Section 907 of the Freedom Support Act, which tied our hands in the early days in Azerbaijan, as well as the tragic war between Azerbaijan and Armenia regarding Nagorno-Karabakh, we have through those two decades supported the development and transportation of Azerbaijani energy resources. Through co-chairmanship of the OSCE Minsk Group, we have provided an opportunity for Armenia and Azerbaijan to pursue a peaceful settlement of the conflict on Nagorno-Karabakh. And we have, especially since 9/11, engaged Azerbaijan in NATO and other international peacekeeping operations in Afghanistan and Kosovo.

I am not saying this has been easy, especially when the United States has pressed Azerbaijan on democracy and human rights issues, but we are in a different place today. There has been a deterioration in U.S.-Azerbaijani relations. Part of this is due to external factors. The changing global energy situation means that Azerbaijan energy resources are less important today than they were in the 1990s, when I was Ambassador. Unfortunately, the Minsk Group has not led to Yerevan and Baku finding the political support to produce a peaceful settlement to the Nagorno-Karabakh situation. And as the U.S. and NATO presence draws down in Afghanistan, Azerbaijan's strategic role in protecting that northern supply route will be less over time. And finally, there has been increased international, not just U.S., focus on human rights and democracy in Azerbaijan.

I think the far more important reasons for the deterioration are internal. There has been an attack on the double-standard the U.S. uses in its approach to the Ukrainian crisis compared to Nagorno-Karabakh. There has been a continued stress of unfairness of U.S. policy with sanctions under 907 of the Freedom Support Act compared to the assistance that we give to Armenia and to the regime in Stepanakert, Nagorno-Karabakh. There is a belief that the U.S. and Europe need Azerbaijani energy more today than Azerbaijan needs the kind of political support we provided in the 1990s and early 2000s to transporting these resources to market.

Our continued support for U.S. NGOs in has increasingly been seen as a negative and led, I think, to this wave of over 90 arrests and detention of Azerbaijanis who are opposing the regime.

Global attacks, unprecedented during my time, on U.S. Government officials, including Ambassadors and the President of the United States have intensified. And we have mentioned the closure of the RFE/RL offices.

As Dr. Altstadt pointed out, I am focused on the December 3 statement by Ramiz Mehtiyev as indicating an end of the era of co-operation between the United States that was established during the presidency of Heydar Aliyev. Accusing the United States of fomenting color revolutions or creating PIF columns is not positive grounds for a good relationship.

So, what can we do under these circumstances? I think it is time to set not a strategic partnership, but a limited set of attainable goals, support serious engagement by both Yerevan and Baku in reaching a negotiated settlement to the Nagorno-Karabakh conflict, support stability in Azerbaijan by all means, but only through greater democracy and observance of international human rights standards, and release the political prisoners. Only then is it possible to talk about a strategic partnership.

If we do not have progress in these areas, then I think it is time to consider sanctions, including travel and other sanctions on officials who are responsible for the arrest and detention of political prisoners, and consider a travel warning to Americans contemplating travel to Azerbaijan.

I think we have reached the point in our relationship that it is time to be concerned about the people. That is why the release of the political prisoners is so important. These prisoners and their families and the American citizens, some of whom are here today, and their families deserve that kind of attention in our relationship that we have not given up to this point.

Thank you.

[The prepared statement of Ambassador Kauzlarich follows:]

Testimony on Azerbaijan

House Foreign Affairs Committee

Subcommittee on Europe, Eurasia and Emerging Threats

Ambassador (ret) Richard D. Kauzlarich

Co-Director Center on Energy Science and Policy

School of Policy, Government and International Affairs

George Mason University

Introduction

Mr. Chairman, I thank the Subcommittee for the opportunity to comment on Azerbaijan. I have had over two decades of experience with the South Caucasus -- as a senor Foreign Service Officer and Ambassador, a think tank and intelligence analyst, and an academic teaching at the graduate level on the geopolitics of energy security. I was U.S. Ambassador in Azerbaijan for three years and have been back several times to observe elections and to train local non-government organization (NGO) representatives in conflict resolution skills.

I commend the Committee for holding these hearings. Azerbaijan and US relations are at a critical point because of human rights violations and the conflict with Armenia regarding Nagorno-Karabakh.

Background

The period of engagement with Azerbaijan since the breakup of the Soviet Union has been a remarkable success for US diplomacy. From my first visit to Baku in 1992 until today, many positive changes in our relations have taken place. This despite the unfair limits imposed on US Government (USG) assistance by Section 907 of the Freedom Support Act of 1992 (FSA907), and the intense conflict with Armenia over the Nagorno-Karabakh region of Azerbaijan.

Both Azerbaijani officials and some US-based analysts argue that the US lacks a coherent policy toward Azerbaijan. I disagree. For two decades, the United States has pursued the following bipartisan policy objectives in Azerbaijan.

- Support the Government of Azerbaijan in maintaining its independence and territorial integrity.
- End the military conflict between Armenia and Azerbaijan regarding Nagorno-Karabakh and, through the Minsk Group process of the Organization for Security and Cooperation in Europe (OSCE), support Azerbaijan and Armenia in achieving a peaceful, negotiated settlement.
- Encourage US commercial interests in the production and transportation of Azerbaijan's substantial energy resources to global markets.

- Work for closer Azerbaijani relations with transatlantic institutions such as the OSCE and North Atlantic Treaty Organization (NATO); and stronger economic relationships with the European Union (EU).
- Strengthen the commitment of Azerbaijan to (1) implementing internationally recognized principles of democracy and human rights; while (2) adopting transparent approaches to governance that minimize corruption.

Azerbaijan and its people have benefited from this US policy and those similar policies of our European allies including Turkey.

- Thanks to USG political support and US energy companies pursuing their commercial interests, the Azerbaijan energy sector has enjoyed enormous success. From the signing of the Contract of the Century in 1994 to the completion of the Baku-Tbilisi-Ceyhan (BTC) pipeline in 2005, US leadership has been critical. Azerbaijan has earned tens of billions of dollars from these energy resources.
- The OSCE Minsk Group process has provided a venue for mediating direct contacts between Baku and Yerevan to conclude peacefully this tragic and painful conflict regarding Nagorno-Karabakh.
- Increased Azerbaijani engagement since the September 11 attack on the US in the international community's priorities of dealing with international terrorism, and participating in NATO-led peace making activities in Kosovo, Iraq and Afghanistan.

This progress was not easy. FSA 907 prohibited direct USG assistance to the Government of Azerbaijan -- unlike its neighbors Armenia and Georgia -- in those early days when institutions and attitudes toward good governance, democracy, and human rights were being developed. Azerbaijanis saw this as unfair treatment of Azerbaijan especially compared to Armenia.

Regarding the Nagorno-Karabakh conflict, as the Minsk Group process produced no results favorable to Azerbaijan, USG positions on resolving the conflict were contrasted with USG positions vis-à-vis the Balkans and more recently Ukraine/Crimea.

Finally US pressure to hold more democratic elections and observe international human rights standards clashed with leadership desires to preserve stability – as they saw it -- and political power.

Times are Changing

Many observers have noticed deterioration in the tone and, in some respects, the substance of US – Azerbaijan relations, especially since the flawed Azerbaijani presidential elections in the fall of 2013. Part of this reflects fundamental shifts in the global and regional political and economic environment.

- The global energy markets have changed profoundly over the past two decades. Global oil and gas production especially in North America has reduced the significance of gas and oil from the Caspian region, and in particular Azerbaijan. The potential energy resources in Azerbaijan are not as great as they appeared in 1994. Gas has replaced oil as the high demand (for energy security reasons) hydrocarbon. Unlike in the 1990s, energy development is being determined more on commercial terms than political priorities as applied when the BTC pipeline was developed.
- Despite the dedication of talented US Minsk Group negotiators, neither Baku nor Yerevan has negotiated directly in a manner leading to a peaceful settlement of this conflict. The leadership in Yerevan and Baku has not prepared their respective publics to accept the compromises that must accompany a negotiated settlement. Further there have been attempts to hold the Minsk Group responsible for finding a solution acceptable to one side and imposing it on the other side. The longer the impasse in the Minsk Group continues the greater the risk of resumed armed conflict. We are at such a point today.
- As the US and NATO drawdown in Afghanistan continues, the importance of Azerbaijan and its neighbors in securing the northern supply route to Afghanistan diminishes. Also Iran's greater engagement in its quest for a nuclear agreement with the West has reduced the security priority accorded to Azerbaijan in that context.
- International support for the observance of human rights and promotion of democracy in Azerbaijan has increased in recent years. At the same time, Azerbaijani support for its international obligations in this area has waned. From the US and Europe, private and official voices have been raised about why after two decades of prosperous stability in Azerbaijan, elections still are not conducted in a free and fair manner, the number of political prisoners has increased, religious freedom is restricted, and freedom of expression shut down.

While such external factors play a role in this deterioration, the most critical factors flow from choices the Baku regime is making for its own reasons, including:

- Frustration over the lack of Western support for the Azerbaijani position on return of Nagorno-Karabakh to Baku's full sovereign control, while supporting Ukraine's position on the return of Crimea to Ukraine.
- Unfairness of FSA 907 while the USG provides economic assistance to Armenia and Nagorno-Karabakh
- With the extraordinary growth of Azerbaijan's energy revenue, Azerbaijan now has the resources including financing and access to technology that it depended on Western companies and governments to provide in the 1990s. It no longer "needs" US and Western political support in the energy arena.
- Lack of respect for Azerbaijan's support for US/NATO efforts especially in Afghanistan, the global fight against terror, and standing up to Iran. Failure of

the US to provide lethal capabilities that Azerbaijan could use in its confrontation with Armenia.

- Concern about internal political instability and the imagined role of US assistance and foreign NGOs and media outlets in supporting the political opposition. Anti-regime demonstrations in Baku and elsewhere in the country in 2013 called attention to corruption, mistreatment of draftees in the Azerbaijani military, and unlawful detention and arrest of opposition politicians, NGO representatives and reporters.
- In particular following the flawed Presidential elections in 2013, the regime began attacking US officials for promoting anti-regime activities. The persons targeted included congressional staffers, US ambassadors (bilateral and Minsk Group co-chair), and finally the President of the United States.
- The shutdown of US NGOs such as IREX and the National Democratic Institute (NDI), and information services including Radio Free Europe/Radio Liberty (RFE/RL).

This culminated with the December 3, 2014 polemic by Chief of the Presidential Apparatus, Ramiz Mehdiyev. This document accuses the USG of fomenting a color revolution in Azerbaijan through "fifth columns" created by USG assistance to US NGOs and affiliated local NGOs.

End of the Heydar Aliyev Era

I have written elsewhere that I believe the Mehdiyev attack on the US represents the end of the Heydar Aliyev (the current President's father) era – an almost two decade long effort by both the United States and Azerbaijan to improve relations despite differences. During that period there was a public profession from the Azerbaijani side of cooperation with the US and support for internationally recognized standards for democracy and observance of human rights.

More than anything else, the many USG statements about flawed elections and human rights abuses, and critical assessments from some European partners pushed official Baku over the top. I believe that the Azerbaijani decision not to follow Georgia on an explicit path toward closer association with the EU reflected official Baku's assessment that closer engagement with the EU would mean a brighter spotlight on its unacceptable treatment of opposition figures and independent media.

The regime is walking a line between being forced to join Russia's Eurasian Economic Union or rejecting the EU – Azerbaijan's largest market for natural gas exports. Yet, it appears that either Europe or Russia is a more acceptable strategic partner for Azerbaijan than the US as long as Washington advocates on behalf of the 90 plus political prisoners, the NGOs, RFE/RL, and an independent Azerbaijani media.

What Can the US Do?

The US and Azerbaijan are in a different place than just five years ago. There are new global and regional geopolitical realities. The global energy picture in particular has changed making Azerbaijan and the Caspian region less critical to US energy security needs.

Rather than trying to construct an abstract "strategic partnership," we need to establish a limited set of attainable goals. Progress on these goals would determine whether a strategic partnership between the US and Azerbaijan is realistic. These could be:

- Serious engagement between Armenia and Azerbaijan by a specific date leading to a peaceful settlement of the dispute regarding Nagorno-Karabakh, and resumed Track-II unofficial contacts between Armenians and Azerbaijanis.
- Support for stability in Azerbaijan based on Baku's movement toward greater democracy and observance of internationally recognized human rights standards.
- Freedom for the over 90 political prisoners.

Without progress in each of these areas, I fear:

- Resumption of armed conflict between Armenia and Azerbaijan.
- Further internal suppression of the remaining liberal democratic elements in the run-up to the 2015 Parliamentary elections in Azerbaijan.

The US cannot allow that to happen. On the human rights front, there are <u>more political prisoners in Azerbaijan than in Belarus and Russia combined</u>. That is unacceptable. Years of diplomatic engagement have not improved the situation. Recently it has become markedly worse than anything I have observed in my experience with Azerbaijan.

If there is no progress toward release of all these prisoners then the USG should consider imposing travel and other <u>sanctions</u> on those officials responsible for the arrest and continued detention of NGO activists and journalists.

I also believe that as long as there is a risk of surveillance and possible detention or arrest of American citizens in Azerbaijan, the Department of State should issue a travel warning for all Americans planning to travel to Azerbaijan.

Why Should the USG Care about Human Rights in Azerbaijan?

<u>Lately Azerbaijani officials have questioned</u> why the US pays attention to "minor issues" like abuses of human rights when there are far more important areas of concern (e.g. European energy security, Iran, Russia, cooperation on anti-terrorism) that the US should be addressing.

Let's set aside for the moment the obligations Azerbaijan has freely undertaken in the UN, the Council of Europe, and the OSCE.

Human rights are a major US security concern. We support, as we have for two decades, the independence and territorial integrity of Azerbaijan. We are limited in what we can do, however, when the regime in Baku suppresses liberal democratic institutions, arrests those who peacefully oppose the lack of democracy and human rights in Azerbaijan, and creates political and social space for other forces that are more dangerous to real stability in Azerbaijan. Make no mistake: radical Islamists are quickly filling the void. They not only burn American and Israeli flags but also send recruits to fight in Syria. When these fighters return to Azerbaijan they represent not only a threat to Azerbaijan but to US security interests as well. That is why human rights are not minor issues.

Thank you.

Mr. ROHRABACHER. I thank all the witnesses.

I will just lead off on the questions. I will try to keep it to 5 minutes, so we all should have a chance before the votes that come up.

Let me just note, as a former journalist, I am fully aware that, when you restrict people's right to criticize the government, it encourages corruption and it makes it more difficult to solve the problems that exist. So, there is an actual, besides just a principle of believing in freedom of speech, it serves the country which respects freedom of speech and freedom of the press. And I hope our friends in Azerbaijan understand that, can come to understand that, and especially because I am sure that there are people who are patriots in that country who are both in the government and outside the government that want what is best for their country.

The criticism that has been leveled, even here today, was not leveled at trying to say that we don't like Azerbaijan and we think of them as an enemy. No, it is just the opposite. We want to create a pathway, so that 10 years from now we could have had a great relationship with a great country that is serving the purpose of peace and stability as well as protecting the rights of their own people.

Let me ask a little bit about this. We know how Azerbaijan compares to the United States or Great Britain. How does it compare in human rights to Iran, its neighbor? Anybody want to answer that?

[No response.]

Don't all jump in at once. I mean, are there more human rights in Azerbaijan than in Iran, respect for the human rights there? Are there more——

Mr. CORNELL. Well, I think one way of answering that is seeing if people from Azerbaijan go to Iran, or vice versa, to get a breather. And as you know, a lot of people from Iran are buying apartments and the like in Azerbaijan in order to get out of Iran.

I think it also depends on exactly what rights are talking about. Especially if you talk about religious rights, there is absolutely no comparison since Azerbaijan actually protects its people from religious extremism; whereas, Iran does the opposite.

If you talk about other types of rights, you could have less of a——

Mr. ROHRABACHER. When I take a look, and as I mentioned in the opening statement, at the countries, the neighborhood that Azerbaijan is in, this is a very tough neighborhood, and I don't believe that any of those countries demonstrably have more respect for human rights than the Azeris have. That is not an excuse for it, but that is putting it in perspective.

And we should not be singling out Azerbaijan. If we are going to have a solid commitment on human rights, which I believe in, we have to make sure that the people in the Azerbaijani Government know that they are not being singled out with a double-standard.

And so, what about Armenia? It is my understanding that that is still a very repressive government in Armenia. How would you compare the human rights in Azerbaijan with Armenia? Anyone want to jump into that?

Ambassador KAUZLARICH. I have a little problem in comparing, you know, what about some other country. I mean, you can say that there are more political prisoners in Azerbaijan than there are in Russia and Belarus together.

Mr. ROHRABACHER. Okay. But the reason that comparison is made is because, without doing it, comparing it to its neighbors, it is automatically being compared to western Europe and the United States. I mean, automatically, that is our standard. And that may not be fair, unless we are willing to make sure that what we are demanding is of each and every one of those countries in the neighborhood.

Ambassador KAUZLARICH. And are we comparing it in terms of numbers of political prisoners, in numbers of opposition newspapers? I mean, these kinds of comparisons, there is not a recognized factor.

Mr. ROHRABACHER. There is not just one factor. Yes, there is a bunch of factors that play into that.

Did you want to jump into that?

Ms. ALTSTADT. Azerbaijan did join the Council of Europe and has been a signatory to other organizations which entailed that it commit itself to upholding human rights and democratization. And Iran, for example, has not done that.

Mr. ROHRABACHER. Of course.

Ms. ALTSTADT. And so, it is important to note that Azerbaijan made these commitments and has not fulfilled them. That is at the most basic level.

Mr. ROHRABACHER. It is not really better to have a country that just thumbs their nose at anything in the West saying that we don't even respect your basic values that you're trying to push versus another country that says, well, we really believe in those, but, then, they fall far short of reaching the standard. Now those are the two things we face.

Ms. ALTSTADT. That assumes that their signing it says that they are committed to those rights. I don't think we are seeing that.

Mr. ROHRABACHER. Okay. Well, I honestly believe we need to make sure human rights is a major part of our policy, but we have to make sure that governments like Azerbaijan, which have not reached that stage, don't think that we are singling them out because we don't like them for one reason or our Government is being manipulated by somebody who doesn't like them.

About the OSCE, has Azerbaijan agreed or has there been an agreement with Azerbaijan with the OSCE about solving the Nagorno-Karabakh dispute? Have they agreed to allow the OSCE to try to find a solution? And has Armenia done that?

Mr. Ambassador?

Ambassador KAUZLARICH. Yes, Mr. Chairman, the OSCE Minsk Group process, not to be confused with the one we are writing to Ukraine, has been in place for several decades. The United States, France, and Russia are co-chairs as mediators. And I think it is a misunderstanding that sometimes both Armenia and Azerbaijan engage in, as if the Minsk Group itself or the mediators are going to provide a solution. It is really they are providing the mechanism where Azerbaijan and Armenia can engage together in trying to find a peaceful solution to the conflict.

Mr. ROHRABACHER. But both have agreed to that?

Ambassador KAUZLARICH. Both have agreed to the process, but both have also agreed not to really made the political commitment necessary to solve the N–K problem. And that is why there is an impasse today. Neither Baku nor Yerevan have made the kind of commitment to solve the problem.

Mr. ROHRABACHER. I have used up my time.

Mr. Meeks?

Mr. MEEKS. Thank you.

So, we have various diplomats on the ground, as you once were, Mr. Ambassador. They have a wide variety of issues because of what they are focusing on today. We just had a newly-appointed, a newly-confirmed Ambassador last week who should arrive in Baku very shortly.

I will start with asking all of you, what would you say our Embassy needs to do on the ground to help (a) improve the relationship and move things forward, as well as help and move things forward on the human rights front? Because the other concern is, how do the regional dynamics help or hurt the democratic principles of Azerbaijan, as indicated? You know, I don't know whether there has been some influence because of what has taken place in the Ukraine, for example. Does that play a role in it or not? What effect do Azerbaijan's calculations in balancing their positions because of their geographic proximity to Iran and Russian—how do these things play?

Let's start with you, Ambassador.

Ambassador KAUZLARICH. Well, I am not going to say what the new Ambassador should do. [Laughter.]

But I think this tripod that Dr. Cornell described, whatever your judgment is on the effectiveness, has to be in place for U.S. and Azerbaijani relations to go forward. What makes it so difficult for Ambassador Cekuta going in is that, unlike when I went to Azerbaijan, he is facing a less-favorable leadership toward strengthening U.S.-Azerbaijani relations. This Ramiz Mehtiyev piece was very telling in rejecting a lot of the values that President Aliyev has said that he endorsed. So, we are really in a very, very difficult place.

And the regional balance question is not going away. I think they look at Ukraine and say, ''Well, you are trying to convince the Russians to give Ukraine back to—or give Crimea back to Ukraine. Why aren't you forcing Armenia to give Nagorno-Karabakh back to Azerbaijan?'' So, there is an issue, when they look at the world, of a double-standard.

But, you know, the question of balance is going to be there, whatever the leadership, whatever the attitude toward human rights. It is just the neighborhood.

Mr. MEEKS. Dr. Cornell, anything else?

Mr. CORNELL. Yes, thank you for your question.

I would say, first of all, that the problem is not with the Embassy, but with the fact that they don't have the backing from the higher levels of the U.S. Government in making this tripod work. The Embassy cannot do that by itself. The Embassy is not even involved in the talks over Nagorno-Karabakh with Armenia. That is a separate office in the U.S. Government, which is held by a very distinguished but mid-career diplomat. This is not a conflict that has been given the attention it deserves from the higher levels of the U.S. Government, especially if we know that the Russians are constantly involved and really don't want a solution to this.

What I think the Embassy could do is to be more active in understanding the intra-regime politics of Azerbaijan. Dr. Altstadt referred to a pro-Moscow faction in ascendency. There are various parts of the Azerbaijani Government that have different ideas about where the country should go.

The parts of the government, and not only government, but business and society, that don't necessarily want a western orientation very often are the ones that are involved in acts that we disagree with and that are not in conformity with Azerbaijan's international commitments. And sometimes it is done for exactly that purpose. So, we have to know why something is being done if we are going to find a way to respond to it.

Mr. MEEKS. Go ahead, Dr. Altstadt. Go ahead.

Ms. ALTSTADT. Thank you.

I have to say that in the many years I have seen the U.S. Embassy in Baku function, I have continually been impressed by the way that they have paid attention to what is going on inside Azerbaijan, the degree to which Ambassadors have tried to learn and use the Azerbaijani language publicly. And in terms of supporting human rights, many of the Ambassadors have actually visited the families of journalists that are being held in prison, and so on. And so, they have many, many tasks to perform, but I have been really impressed with how well they have functioned in the meantime.

And I think that it is very important to note that, not only the government, but the public in Azerbaijan is extremely sensitive to the way the United States treats Azerbaijan and the other governments in the region and elsewhere. I think the reason for that is that they hold the United States to a higher standard. They expect more of us, and I think that is appropriate and we should live up to that.

Mr. MEEKS. Well, my other question was going to back to Dr. Altstadt also, but I am going to be brief because I know we have got votes coming up.

Because I was wondering about it. I mean, should I take anything out of that 2 weeks ago the Azerbaijani delegation to the Parliamentarian Assembly of the Council of Europe, of course, spoke out for Russia and voted against sanctions for Russia. So, it does seem that Russia and Azerbaijan have exchanged a high-level delegation and launched out to venture to explore oil and gas.

Now is that something that we should look at as far strained relations with the United States? Should that be something that we are concerned with? Or is that just being strategically trying to figure out where that balance is because they live next to this other big country?

Ms. ALTSTADT. I believe in the case of Ilham Aliyev, like with his father Heydar Aliyev, whom he succeeded, that they are striving to find a balance. And at some point they need to do more things to accommodate Russian interests. And so, I find it worrying, on the one hand, that they are doing that. They also applied to join, as observers, to join the Shanghai Cooperation Organization. But, in the larger picture, I think it is part of a tilt toward Russia, but I don't see it as a radical change in direction over the long run.

Mr. ROHRABACHER. Thank you very much.

Mr. Brooks?

Mr. BROOKS. Thank you, Mr. Chairman.

I have been looking at on the internet stats about Azerbaijan. As I understand it, it is roughly a 9.4 million population, of which 95 percent is Islam of one kind or another. As I also understand, its leaders are elected. Is that correct?

Ms. ALTSTADT. There are elections. [Laughter.]

Mr. BROOKS. There are elections? Okay. The way you answered that, what do you mean by ''There are elections.''? Are you telling me that there is a lot of fraud or that there is no competition or there is not more than one party? What do you mean?

Ms. ALTSTADT. All of the international observers that have observed Azerbaijani elections have declared them to be not free and fair, for all of the reasons you suggested: The runup to the election, restrictions on opposition parties, carousel voting, and ballot stuffing during the polling itself, falsifications of every kind.

Mr. BROOKS. Is Azerbaijan now a threat to any other nation? Please.

Ambassador KAUZLARICH. Because of this unresolved conflict regarding the Nagorno-Karabakh region, there is the great threat of a military conflict resuming again with Armenia.

Mr. BROOKS. When was the last time there was a military conflict between Armenia and Azerbaijan?

Ambassador KAUZLARICH. There has been a ceasefire in effect since 1994, Russian-imposed, by the way. But, in recent months, there has been an increase in military action from both the Armenian and the Azeri side, resulting in deaths of military and civilians on both sides.

Mr. BROOKS. And are there any other countries that are threats to, in your judgment, Azerbaijan?

Ms. ALTSTADT. I think Russia is potentially a threat. I think that in more subtle ways Iran is potentially a threat.

But I do want to emphasize, sir, that even though they are a Muslim-majority country, it is highly-secular society, and it has been secular because of indigenous secular movements since the 19th century.

Mr. BROOKS. What do you mean by the phrase ''highly-secular''?

Ms. ALTSTADT. In other words, the degrees to which the people adhere to Islam, the forms that it takes, and the public practice, all are on a very wide range, as we might find in the United States in terms of people who adhere to particular religions, and some go to church every Sunday and some show up faithfully on Christmas Eve. So, there are those kinds of differences.

But the real, I think, politically-important question is political Islam and whether there is a political use of Islam, and that is much less. And even for those situations, the degree to which it is radical is an even smaller amount. It is very difficult to measure, however, because research on that topic is, of course, very sensitive, and it is very difficult for anyone to do.

Mr. BROOKS. My next question may be a little bit difficult for you. But I am from a community that has the highest number of engineers per capita in the United States, a lot of scientists, physicists, highly-educated people who like numbers. And so, I am going to ask you to try to rank on a scale of 1 to 10, where 1 is no substantive relationship to 10 is a great relationship. Now how would you rate today the relations between America and Azerbaijan?

Dr. Altstadt, we will start with you first. On a 1-to-10 scale, give us a feel.

Ms. ALTSTADT. So, 1 is no meaningful relationship and 10——

Mr. BROOKS. Yes, ma'am.

Ms. ALTSTADT [continuing]. Is wonderful relationship?

Mr. BROOKS. Yes, ma'am.

Ms. ALTSTADT. For quality or quantity?

Mr. BROOKS. Quality.

Ms. ALTSTADT. 7, 6.

Mr. BROOKS. A 7. So, it is pretty good? Better than average, in your judgment, the relations between America and Azerbaijan? Five would be average.

Ms. ALTSTADT. Well, let me revise that and say 5.

Mr. BROOKS. 5? Okay, about average.

Dr. Cornell?

Mr. CORNELL. 5.

Ambassador KAUZLARICH. 3½.

Mr. CORNELL. 3½? Why do you say 3½ versus these others who suggest that it is about a normal American versus another country relationship?

Ambassador KAUZLARICH. Because in my two decades' experience there has been no senior Azerbaijani political figure who has written a document that attacks the United States and its leadership. That is not a sign along with accusing us of being involved in fomenting yellow or color revolutions.

Mr. BROOKS. I caught on a comment by Dr. Cornell that America's presence must once again be felt in the region. And as we all know, America has limited resources. We have limited money, limited military. We have engagements all over the world, relationships all over the world.

Why should America divert our limited resources from other hotspots in the world or from other places where we want to have relationships to Azerbaijan? What is our national interest?

Mr. CORNELL. Let me answer that very briefly. I think the first part of the answer is that this is not about money. This is about political leadership and attention, which we used to have, which we don't anymore.

The second part is that the reason is, as I described initially, that you have a country and a region which is a factor in both of the major issues facing the Transatlantic Alliance, which is the expansionism of Russia and the Islamic radicalism of the Middle East. And Azerbaijan and the whole region of the Caucuses in Central Asia is a potential bulwark against both of those.

I will end by saying that the experience of 9/11 showed that cultivating relations with these countries became a crucial asset in prosecuting the war in Afghanistan. Mr. Chairman himself used the word "irreplaceable" for that, the level of support, the air corridor through Azerbaijan, which enabled the U.S. to deploy military resources in Central Asia and Afghanistan.

Mr. BROOKS. Thank you, Mr. Chairman.

Mr. ROHRABACHER. Now we have a vote coming. It is my intent to have the ranking member have his closing statement and, then, the chairman—that's me—will have a closing statement.

Mr. MEEKS. I just want to, you know, because I am trying to be as balanced as we can, because the flip side, I had asked the question about Russia.

Had we had more time, I wanted to ask a question about Iran because the relations between Azerbaijan and Iran have been tough also, and Islamic Republic, they have been capriciously unhappy, I believe, with the secular Azerbaijan and have not spared any effort to undermine its very foundations of Azerbaijan society. And Azerbaijan's close ties with Israel—they have close ties with Israel—and the West have been met with hostility, too, by Iran.

So, as the administration talks to Iran over its nuclear program, you know, if we had time, the question is, how does this engagement influence regional dynamics in the South Caucuses and, in particular, the Iranian policies vis-à-vis Azerbaijan?

Because what I really, if we had time to highlight it, there is pressure. The reason I asked the Russian question is because sometimes in the region, they are a big country in the region, so they have got to figure out how to work with Russia and not just say, ''We are not going to work with them at all.''

On the other side they have got Iran who does not like their relationship. So, they have got to figure out how to live in that world.

So, Azerbaijan is kind of squeezed, you know, in the middle there in trying to determine how they can survive in the middle of these two and, yet, still be a great friend or, as you have said, most of you, an average friend to the United States.

So, I conclude just by saying that we have got to work together. It is important that we work together, that we improve the relationship. And when you are friends and allies, you know, I don't want folks to think that is when you just say, ''Look,'' to your friend, ''I want to help you with whatever deficiencies you have.'' Because I understand, from my perspective, we in the United States still are trying to improve also with reference to our human rights issues that we still have in this country.

Mr. ROHRABACHER. Thank you very much, Mr. Meeks.

We will be going down to the Floor to demonstrate how people with different views can work together.

Well, that was a joke, actually. [Laughter.]

With that said, I think that Azerbaijan is a very significant country to the well-being of the United States and the stability of the world. We wish them well. We think it would be better for them and everybody if they would be, as I say, a little less thin-skinned about criticism and wouldn't go after people because they are criticizing. We recognize that in America as something that helps us perfect ourselves, helps us solve the problems by knowing about them.

But Azerbaijan, we have to make sure that we are not singling out a friendly country which is surrounded by basically countries that aren't necessarily friendly to our interest and friendly to the United States, singling them out to try to attack their flaws in a way that will weaken them in relationship to the others in their neighborhood. This is something that requires a great deal of soul-searching as to where to draw the line.

We appreciate your guidance today from the witnesses on helping us make that decision as to how we will draw that line and set the policy that will stay true to our principles of liberty and justice while still watching out for our national interest to keep a stable part of the world right there. Because if Azerbaijan would go the direction of Iran, and if radical Islam would sweep into Central Asia, the world would not be a decent place to live in 30 years from now or even 20 years from now.

We saw that happen when little nut-cases in Germany took over the government and we ended up in a conflagration. Well, radical Islam poses that same kind of—you know, these are fanatic people, and if they get control of Central Asia as well as perhaps the Middle East, it will be a totally different world, and not a good world.

So, let's work with those people who will work with us. Hopefully, we can nudge our friends to go in the right direction.

So, thank you all for your advice on how to draw that line and achieve that goal.

This hearing is now adjourned.

[Whereupon, at 2:03 p.m., the meeting was adjourned.]

APPENDIX

MATERIAL SUBMITTED FOR THE RECORD

SUBCOMMITTEE HEARING NOTICE
COMMITTEE ON FOREIGN AFFAIRS
U.S. HOUSE OF REPRESENTATIVES
WASHINGTON, D.C. 20515-6128

Subcommittee on Europe, Eurasia, and Emerging Threats
Dana Rohrabacher (R-CA), Chairman

February 5, 2015

TO: MEMBERS OF THE COMMITTEE ON FOREIGN AFFAIRS

You are respectfully requested to attend an OPEN hearing of the Committee on Foreign Affairs, to be held by the Subcommittee on Europe, Eurasia, and Emerging Threats in Room 2200 of the Rayburn House Office Building (and available on the Committee website at www.foreignaffairs.gov):

DATE: Thursday, February 12, 2015

TIME: 1:00 p.m.

SUBJECT: Azerbaijan: U.S. Energy, Security, and Human Rights Interests

WITNESSES: Audrey Altstadt, Ph.D.
                   Fellow
                   Kennan Institute
                   Woodrow Wilson International Center for Scholars

                   The Honorable Richard Kauzlarich
                   Adjunct Professor
                   School of Public Policy
                   George Mason University
                   (Former American Ambassador to Azerbaijan)

                   Svante Cornell, Ph.D.
                   Director
                   Central Asia-Caucasus Institute
                   School of Advanced International Studies
                   Johns Hopkins University

By Direction of the Chairman

The Committee on Foreign Affairs seeks to make its facilities accessible to persons with disabilities. If you are in need of special accommodations, please call 202/225-5021 at least four business days in advance of the event, whenever practicable. Questions with regard to special accommodations in general (including availability of Committee materials in alternative formats and assistive listening devices) may be directed to the Committee.

COMMITTEE ON FOREIGN AFFAIRS

MINUTES OF SUBCOMMITTEE ON _____ *Europe, Eurasia, and Emerging Threats* _____ HEARING

Day___ *Thursday* ___Date___ *February 12, 2015* ___Room___ *Rayburn 2200* ___

Starting Time ___ *1:00pm* ___Ending Time ___ *2:03pm* ___

Recesses |___| (___to___) (___to___) (___to___) (___to___) (___to___) (___to___)

Presiding Member(s)

Rep. Dana Rohrabacher

Check all of the following that apply:

Open Session ☑   Electronically Recorded (taped) ☑
Exécutive (closed) Session ☐   Stenographic Record ☑
Televised ☑

TITLE OF HEARING:

Azerbaijan: U.S. Energy, Security, and Human Rights Interests

SUBCOMMITTEE MEMBERS PRESENT:

Rep. Meeks, Rep. Brooks, Rep. Sires, Rep. Deutch, Rep. Keating.

NON-SUBCOMMITTEE MEMBERS PRESENT: *(Mark with an * if they are not members of full committee.)*

HEARING WITNESSES: Same as meeting notice attached? Yes ☑ No ☐
(If "no", please list below and include title, agency, department, or organization.)

STATEMENTS FOR THE RECORD: *(List any statements submitted for the record.)*

Congressman Michael Turner
Congressman Michael Fitzpatrick

TIME SCHEDULED TO RECONVENE _____
or
TIME ADJOURNED ___ *2:03* ___

Subcommittee Staff Director

MATERIAL SUBMITTED FOR THE RECORD BY THE HONORABLE DANA ROHRABACHER, A
REPRESENTATIVE IN CONGRESS FROM THE STATE OF CALIFORNIA, AND CHAIRMAN,
SUBCOMMITTEE ON EUROPE, EURASIA, AND EMERGING THREATS

MICHAEL R. TURNER
TENTH DISTRICT, OHIO

COMMITTEE ON ARMED SERVICES
CHAIRMAN
SUBCOMMITTEE ON
TACTICAL AIR AND LAND FORCES

COMMITTEE ON OVERSIGHT AND
GOVERNMENT REFORM

ASSISTANT MAJORITY WHIP

2239 RAYBURN HOUSE OFFICE BUILDING
WASHINGTON, DC 20515
(202) 225-6465

DISTRICT OFFICE:

120 WEST 3RD STREET
SUITE 305
DAYTON, OH 45402
(937) 225-2843

Congress of the United States
House of Representatives
Washington, DC 20515
February 12, 2015

Statement for the Record
The Honorable Michael R. Turner
House Committee on Foreign Affairs
Subcommittee on Europe, Eurasia, and Emerging Threats
"Azerbaijan: U.S. Energy, Security, and Human Rights Interests"

Chairman Rohrabacher, Ranking Member Meeks, and Members of the Subcommittee, thank you
for the opportunity to submit a statement for the record for this hearing.

Azerbaijan continues to be an important partner with the United States in efforts to bolster
geopolitical energy security. With its vast resources of oil and natural gas, Azerbaijan is a key
component to help our strategic allies in the North Atlantic Treaty Organization and other
European partners to diversify their energy resources.

As you know, the Baku-Tbilisi-Ceyhan (BTC) oil pipeline runs from the Caspian Sea through
Azerbaijan, Georgia, and Turkey. This multi-national initiative, which garnered support from
the United States, helps diversify global oil resources and fosters closer geopolitical relationships
in the region. Since it became operational in 2006, the BTC pipeline has carried approximately
2.03 billion barrels of crude oil to the global oil marketplace.

Mr. Chairman, opening the Southern Gas Corridor is another critically important component to
help our European allies diversify their energy resources. As you know, successive U.S.
Administrations have expressed support for this project as a means to provide new energy supply
routes for Europe. The Southern Gas Corridor, which will transit Azerbaijan, Georgia, Turkey,
Greece, Albania, and Italy, is expected to carry 16 billion cubic meters per year of natural gas
from the Caspian Sea to Europe beginning in 2018/2019.

While this amount represents less than five percent of current European consumption, the
Southern Gas Corridor will allow Europe to access alternative and reliable sources of energy,
helping to provide our allies with greater market choice. In addition, the establishment of this
pipeline lays the foundation for opportunities for greater amounts of natural gas production,
increased pipeline infrastructure development, and enhanced regional cooperation to bring
additional energy resources to our transatlantic allies.

Mr. Chairman, as we have seen recently in Europe, access to diverse energy supplies is critical to
fostering economic security, maintaining independence, and curbing the use of energy as a
political weapon. The United States must continue to work with Azerbaijan to help strengthen
European energy security and promote regional stability.

Congressman Mike Fitzpatrick
Statement for the Record

The Republic of Azerbaijan has been an important partner and ally to the United States in recent years, through military cooperation and energy exploration and development. The U.S.-Azerbaijani relationship has been positive for both countries, which makes the recent news coming from Baku all the more disappointing.

The recent government crackdown on free speech is an inexcusable false step for the Azerbaijani government.

A constituent of mine, Sarah Paulsworth informed me of a current situation regarding her husband, Emin Huseynov, who has spent the last six months hiding from his own government. Emin is a founding member of the Institute for Reporters' Freedom and Safety, a legally registered NGO in Azerbaijan. This past August, IRFS was raided by Azerbaijani officials and Emin was declared "wanted" by law enforcement due to a alleged charge regarding tax evasion. Emin is currently residing in the Swiss embassy in Baku, waiting for an opportunity to leave Azerbaijan.

I have reached out to both the Department of State and the Azerbaijani Ambassador to the U.S., advocating for Emin's case. Today I wish to, once again, call on the Republic of Azerbaijan to withdraw charges against Emin Huseynov and grant him safe passage out of the country, so he may be reunited with his wife.